7.53

THE
FLAMING
CENTER

THE
FLAMING
CENTER

A Theology of the Christian Mission

CARL E. BRAATEN

FORTRESS PRESS   Philadelphia

Library of Congress Catalog Card Number 76–62605

ISBN 0–8006–0490–3

6191C77   Printed in U.S.A.   1–490

CONTENTS

INTRODUCTION

For a long time I have waited for the chance to write a theology of mission. The right time seemed to become ever more distant as the literature on the subject grew by leaps and bounds. My travels around the world during 1974–1975 made the prospect seem even dimmer, since it revealed the gap between the magnitude of the task and my readiness for it. Nevertheless, I have written this book on the mission of the gospel in the world, even though the time is not ripe and I never felt ready. But I do not wish to wait forever.

I have wanted to bring together thoughts I had gained both from a theological trip into the labyrinth of eschatology and from reflections on my existential origins in the laboratory of mission. For I was born of missionary parents. That is the deepest and most enduring datum of my own self-understanding—as a human being and as a Christian. As a theologian I gradually became aware of the alliance between eschatology and mission in the Bible and in the history of Christianity. As a result my head and my heart have both been at work on this essay toward a theology of the Christian mission in world history, though the contributions of the heart remain mostly latent. After all, this is a *theology* of mission, and not a personal diary.

Mission is understood as the function of the kingdom of God in world history. The church has its role in the scheme of eschatology, and that is to serve as God's agent for mission. The church has inherited from Israel the consciousness of being the people of God elected for mission. This little ditty by Ogden Nash applies to the church too:

> How odd of God
> To choose the Jews.

But how should we relate the kingdom of God, the church, and the world

1

in a theology of mission? The answer is not new; it is as old as the gospel. The flaming center of the Christian message is Jesus, the Christ of God, the Savior of mankind and the Lord of history. Our overriding concern is to remind the church of its task to proclaim this message to all the nations until the end of history.

There are some recurring themes to which we might call attention in advance. We are pleading for an expanding horizon of the gospel in today's world. Nothing less than the universal gospel will meet the needs of the human condition we experience today. The world is lapsing into a kind of polydemonism in which false particularisms are being lifted up like a brazen serpent as ultimately worthy of the incense of human loyalty.

There are many demons to be named and driven out to make way for the mission of the universal gospel. One such demon is the retreat to ahistorical mysticism in religion. This abstract kind of mysticism always promises a universal viewpoint, but it flees like the devil from the concrete universal embodied in the person of Jesus Christ. A second demon is the recourse to subjective experience as source and norm of theology, in exchange for the creative power of the biblical word. A third demon is the retrenchment of the church in society, its pulling back from daring ventures, seeking security behind a wall of separation and consolation in the old-time religion. A fourth demon is a relapse into legalism in morality, preferring the precedents of law to the uncharted course of freedom. A fifth demon is the resurgence of nationalism in world affairs, spreading even to the Olympic Games.

All these demons promise people a piece of salvation. But in the end they are bound to fail; they grant universal significance to particular things. Idolatry is the biblical name for this operation. The Christian message runs in the opposite direction. The universal has become concrete in the person of Jesus Christ. The Word has become flesh; the kingdom of God has become history. *Incarnation* is the theological term for this event.

Mission is the process of exploring the universal significance of the gospel in history. It began when the Jews—a particular people—got the idea that their God is the Lord of all the nations. They believed in the universality of their God, but they did not make it their mission to preach to the nations. Paul was the one who took the mission to the nations, believing that the resurrected Christ commanded his disciples to bring salvation to the uttermost parts of the earth. When Christianity hit Greek soil, the challenge was to demonstrate the universal truth of Christ in dialogue with Greek philosophy and to outthink the pagan philosophers. In the fourth century Christianity became the established religion of the Roman Empire. The church acquired political significance, playing a constructive role in the development of medieval culture. Thus, in religion, philosophy, and culture the church discovered new ways of expanding its understanding of the faith.

The modern period confronted the church with new challenges. At first Christian theologians fought with science, then baptized it, and finally dicovered that the whole scientific enterprise presupposes a Christian view of the world as creation. On Christian soil the universal spirit took off into commerce and colonialism. There was a kind of missionary motive in bringing the blessings of civilization to savages living in darkness. Capitalism thought of itself as the Christian form of economics, based on a biblical doctrine of man and society. The Christian West spread the faith to all the nations, translated the Bible into hundreds of dialects, and planted the church in virtually every land, so that now Christianity is by far the most universal of all the major religions.

It is common to say that we are now living in postmodern times. New challenges have arisen to test the universal meaning of the gospel. When the church successfully meets a challenge, the door of history opens and the church goes forward in mission. Otherwise the door is shut and the church runs the risk of becoming a religious sect. Today Christianity is being challenged by Marxism to develop the social implications of its message. If the Lord is risen and the gospel is true, we have unplumbed resources to expand the mission for peace and justice and the general promotion of human welfare and world community.

We refuse to take sides in the polarization between evangelical-minded and ecumenical-minded theologians who needlessly restrict the gospel either to its vertical dimension of personal salvation through faith in Jesus Christ or its horizontal dimension of human liberation through the creation of a just social order. It is painful to hear leading evangelicals sneer at the concerns of the ecumenical people who connect mission to liberation, revolution, humanization, dialogue, secularization, socialization, and the like.   For the deepest human longings and profoundest social needs are gathered up and reflected in such slogans.   To dismiss them to a place of secondary importance is to pass by on the other side, while modern man lies in the ditch bleeding to death.   It is equally disturbing when ecumenical voices fail to find the language to underscore the permanent relevance of gospel proclamation in sermon and sacraments, in words of witness as well as deeds which lead to personal conversion and the spread of Christianity.   In stressing now the social dimensions of the gospel we do not diminish one bit its depth dimension in personal life and the *koinonia* of faith and worship.   A theology of the gospel includes personal salvation and human liberation.   It includes both forgiveness and freedom, both faith and food.   As one slogan puts it: God is not dead; God is bread!

The universal gospel is the only answer to the polydemonism which works destructively to fragment the world and sets its pieces in conflict over competing ultimate loyalties.   Salvation in Christ is the power of wholeness, overcoming the splitting of reality in both public and private manifestations.   Such wholeness should reflect itself in the unity of the church.   Here lies the urgency of the unfinished ecumenical agenda. The world does not need Christianity as one more religion or ideology to engage in splitting an already badly fractured world.   Polarization in the churches happens when the gods of this world enter the body of Christ, setting its members at odds with each other.   So the health of the one body and its unified mission in a broken world suffers serious impairment.   The problem lies in the fragmentation of the gospel itself, neutralizing its claim to speak for the Lordship of Jesus in our bodily and earthly life here and now, in all its social, political, and economic dimensions.

We have touched on another theme that runs throughout this book, a critique of a two-kingdoms doctrine that has worked special mischief in the Reformation tradition.   Dichotomizing the kingdom of God confines the church and its message to a narrow religious base of operation uncharacteristic of biblical religion.   Nothing has been more destructive of the church's mission than impaling it on one side of a series of dualistic antitheses.   There was the old Greek dualism of body and soul. Some ancient Christians adopted it and assigned the gospel to the soul. No less harmful was the medieval dualism between nature and grace, whereby it became necessary to relegate the operations of grace to a supernatural plane. Pietism, from which most of the modern missionary movements stem, dichotomized between individual and society, religion and culture, evangelism and social welfare. Although we have aimed to destroy all these false dichotomies, we have not surrendered the dualistic factor that goes hand in hand with the eschatological qualification of history and existence we find in the New Testament.

Christianity is an eschatological faith. There is a sense, to be sure, in which every religion carries an implicit eschatology of some kind. It is the essence of religion to call for the end of the world as we know it and to promise by means of myth, magic, or mystery a new beginning. The presupposition of religion is that the world as we ordinarily perceive it appears old when compared to the new that religion makes possible. True, the new may be thought of as renewal, but still new compared to the old that is now present. There would be no need for religion were there no human predicament.

In some religions the eschatology in question is nonhistorical. The contrast between the new and the old, good and evil, salvation and damnation has nothing to do with history. Everything is placed on a vertical line between God and the world. Mysticism is the religion that fits this vertical line the best. The temporal aspects of past, present, and future in the structure of history have no real significance for the way in which God reveals himself and saves the world. The important thing is mystical experience going on inside the soul.

There are other religions which can be placed on a horizontal line. Such religions live in the present with memories of the past and hopes for the future. They seek to penetrate not only the soul of the individual but also the life of society. Their way is not to climb a mystical ladder of salvation leading to heaven but to wrestle with the powers that be and the principalities of world history. This horizontal line is represented by Jewish, Christian, and Marxist interpretations of history, each of which follows a basic Hebraic outlook.

The fact that Christianity is a religion of the concrete universal means that the vertical and horizontal lines intersect in Jesus of Nazareth in a special way.   Christianity inherited from its Jewish mother the history of promise pointing to the future.   Israel reported this history at two levels: at the historical level of her existence amidst the nations of the world, and at the universal level where she becomes the paradigm of the divine-human encounter.   Israel's story becomes a microhistory within the macrodrama of the creation and redemption of the world.   Consequently, in Jewish apocalyptic eschatology the history of promise that points to the future holds together both a vision of the future *in* history for Israel as well as the future *of* history for the whole world.   Israel looked to the future for the coming of salvation, for herself, for the whole of humanity, and finally for the entire cosmos.

The core problem in a theology of mission that can deal holistically with the soteriological and the sociological thrusts of the gospel has to do with the way in which eschatology and history are tied in with each other.   It is not enough to have an eschatology; nor is it enough to take history seriously.   We need to be clear on how they are related and how they are not related to each other.   The clue for us lies not in a general metaphysics of history, but in the preaching of Jesus and the message of primitive Christianity.   The New Testament reports that something decisive happened in history, which, if true, defines not only the essence of Christianity but the shape of its mission to the nations.

The promise of the future that points to the end of history is identified with the person of Jesus, although he stands smack in the middle of history.   The eschatological future of the world becomes present in the person of Jesus without as yet bringing history to an end. This is the claim of the gospel: the personal future of everyone and the universal future of the world are linked to the eschatological event hiddenly present in the life, death, and resurrection of Jesus of Nazareth.   But history goes on as a time for mission—to bring the gospel to the nations in all its scope and power.   The language of the future becomes dualized, and here is the dualistic factor mentioned above.   We can speak of the eschatological future that is *already* present through faith in Christ and the future that has *not yet* taken the world home to its final destiny in God.   Mission exists in the tension-creating distinction between the "already" and the "not-yet" in the eschatological kingdom at work in history.   This kind of historico-eschatological dualism is totally different from the metaphysical dualism which infiltrated Christian faith through gnosticism and Neo-Platonic philosophy.

Those who wish to go beyond a theology of mission to the practical problems of how to do the mission in the many contexts of today's world will necessarily be disappointed by the meagre suggestions in this book. We have not been able to offer concrete proposals on mission strategy for our time. To be concrete and practical one has to live one's way into the context in question and be as specific as possible in relation to local conditions. What one would say for Africa would hardly apply in South America. One can hardly even speak of neighboring countries like Kenya and Tanzania in the same breath. What goes for India would not hold for China. Hong Kong is not Singapore. Generalities on mission strategy become superficial to the point of absurdity in face of the contextual complexities and variations that rise up to challenge a theology of mission. Yet, I am not persuaded that we need to be captivated by a thoroughgoing regionalization of theology, as though what is theologically adequate in America would be theologically irrelevant in Africa. I would hope that even those who are rightly working most vigorously for the Africanization of theology, as John S. Mbiti is doing, would be able to recognize in our effort the validity of what we call "the flaming center" for a theology of mission valid for all six continents. I would forcefully deny that conditions could arise in time or exist anywhere in space such as to nullify or neutralize the universal historical power and everlasting truth of the gospel of Jesus Christ. Where such conditions do seem to exist, the task of the church's mission is clearly to change them.

I have acknowledged the importance of liberation as a new focus for the church's mission. But I am unable to give a ringing endorsement to any particular brand of liberation theology. The theme of liberation belongs to the gospel. This should keep us free from the temptation to take it into ideological captivity where the vision of Marx outweighs the message of Jesus. Some will say I have conceded too much to the spirit of the times embodied in the language of liberation, others that I have not escaped the bondage that is called "North Atlantic Christianity." Perhaps both are right—or neither. The words of Shakespeare in *Hamlet* keep coming back: "This above all, to thine own self be true; and then it must follow as the night from day, thou canst not be false to any man." Yet it is not so much the desire to be true to self as to be faithful to the gospel that shapes our "yes and no" to liberation theology.

Finally, I must confess that I am awed but not persuaded by recent speculations, especially among Roman Catholic theologians like Karl Rahner, H.R. Schlette, and Raimundo Panikkar, on how broad the way of salvation is in the world religions, apart from the revelation of God in the history of Israel and Jesus of Nazareth. It is comforting, of course, to know that after all there is salvation outside the Roman Catholic Church, but to spread what we mean by Christ or by church so thin that it can be found anywhere and everywhere is a choice dictated more by a medieval conception of "nature and grace" than by the New Testament message of Jesus and the primitive Christian mission. The universal promise which belongs to the gospel as its inmost hope waits upon the eschatological Christ and his role in the final kingdom of God for its realization. The task is not so much to show how the world religions can work salvation by the grace of God, but how the church's mission can lure them into the openness of world history where they might encounter the message of Christ, which alone can promise the fulfillment for which they have been groping. This refusal to violate the New Testament canon of "no other gospel" and "no other name" would seem to place me on the side of the evangelical theologians. That is true with respect to the christological focus. But I am unable to abandon the integrity of the universal promise which looks beyond "my personal faith" to an eschatological resolution that only God in his final mercy can determine. The finality of his judgment has already been previewed in the death of Jesus which spells mercy for all—there is reason not to abandon hope for every last sinner and for the whole world. This is a universalism of agape, of hope against hope, which for us lies not at the speculative periphery of the gospel, but at its flaming center.

1

MISSION: THE MOTHER OF CHRISTIAN THEOLOGY

THE DOUBLE TASK OF THEOLOGY

In 1930 William Ernest Hocking headed up a commission to examine the missionary enterprise of American Protestantism. The report of this commission, entitled *Re-Thinking Missions*, spoke of the Christian mission as having come to a fork in the road. Since the earliest days of mission in the New Testament the Christian faith has spread throughout the world on the preaching of "one way of salvation and one only."[1] The core of its message has always been, the report admits, the "essential paradox, the universal claim of one particular historic fact: the work of Christ."[2] The original aim of the Christian mission was "to proclaim truth, which is universal; but its truth was embodied in a particular person and His work."[3] This central claim of universal truth through the particular revelation of God in Christ can no longer be sustained, the 1930 report said, as the driving force of the Christian mission. Hence we come to a fork in the road. We are asked to rid Christianity of that exclusivist element of the gospel that announces the salvation of mankind through "no other Name" than that of Jesus Christ. How can we expect a universal result from one particular fact of history? The renewal of the Christian mission calls for a broadening of its base so that it stands "upon the common ground of all religion"[4] and joins all others in the search for the final truth which is "the New Testament of every existing faith."[5] The report clearly pointed out the difference between the old way of mission which follows "but one way, the way of Christ" and the new way which aims at a partnership with all other religions in "a common search for truth."[6] The churches are now back at the same fork in the road. The challenge to be relevant in mission on a worldwide scale is frequently coupled with a demand that

9

Christianity abandon its narrow belief that Jesus Christ is the Savior of all mankind.

The most explicit recent challenge to the christic core of the gospel has been set forth by John Hick in his book entitled *God and the Universe of Faiths*. From the beginning, Hick says, Christianity has traditionally held that "salvation is through Christ alone."[7] Hick himself held this same belief for twenty-five years. Then he came to know personally people of other faiths and discovered that he no longer could believe that their lack of faith in Christ would count against their chance of salvation. As the Hocking report placed the churches at the fork in the road, asking them to level down the place of Jesus to that of other great founders of religion, so Hick is calling for a "Copernican revolution in theology" which removes Christianity from the center of the universe of faiths to the circumference where it revolves, not around the gospel of Christ, but along with the other religions around *God* who is at the center.[8]

If on the religious front, then, Christianity would gain a greater relevance by placing Jesus in line with Buddha and Mohammed, why not do a similar thing on the social front? Why not place Jesus on the level of the social prophets of our era, with Marx, Lenin, and Mao Tse-Tung? Or with Che Guevara, Malcolm X, and any other great revolutionary leader who tells people what to believe and do? The challenge on both fronts, the religious and the social, is fundamental; it goes to the heart of the Christian mission. It has to do with the basis and content of Christian faith. It is a question of the essence of Christianity. Nothing less than the identity of the Christian church is at stake in the challenge to seek greater relevance for Christianity to the modern world by levelling down the place of Jesus to that of the great religious personalities and social prophets of world history.

The gospel of Jesus Christ, and nothing else, is the identity principle of Christianity. This sounds like a very dogmatic assertion, but nothing else could possibly qualify as such in light of the facts of history. This gospel is also the very thing by which Christianity seeks to be relevant in world history. The gospel is the central datum of mission. If dialogue is a new form of mission in the Christian encounter with other religions, this is a gain over the past era. But the material question of what Christianity has to say as its part in the dialogue is: What is the gospel of Jesus Christ? In two thousand years of Christian tradition, there are many topics of interest that can be placed on the agenda of the inter-religious dialogue, but compared to the one thing burning in the heart of the Christian witness, namely, the conviction that "the Lord has risen indeed" (Luke 24:34) such things do not come close to revealing the inner identity of the Christian faith. Turning the matter around, if representatives of other religions in dialogue with Christians were to beat around the bush and not disclose what lies within the inner sanctum of their own religion, they would be wasting our time. Worse, they would be deceiving us. Accordingly, if Christians are not to withhold from their partners in dialogue what for them stands at the sacred center of faith, they will have to become clear about the gospel of Jesus Christ. Only then can they explain to others the secret of the Christian mis-sion. For mission is not a program added on to the gospel, but is fundamental to its very nature.

We must seek to find the missionary relevance of Christianity once again in its evangelical identity. Churches are being called to re-pentance for having exhibited too much apostolic zeal over the wrong things. When missionaries are told to go home, is it the gospel they are asked to take back with them, or merely those epiphenomena of mission that do not necessarily emanate from the ground of the gospel? Can the mission of the gospel be liberated from false dependencies on dated Western forms?

The task of theology is twofold: to inquire about the nature of the gospel, and to ask whether the praxis of mission truly reflects the faith. Where the identity of Christianity is found in the gospel of Jesus Christ, there the mission of the church arises as universally relevant—"unto the ends of the earth and until the end of the world." The question is not whether Christianity is the best religion on earth or whether it should launch a mission here or there, either from the urge to express itself or to solve the problems of the world. Emil Brunner once said, "The Church exists by mission, just as fire exits by burning. Where there is no mission, there is no Church; and where there is neither Church nor mission, there is no faith."[9]   The very identity of Christianity in the gospel of Christ makes it by nature a messianic movement with a universal historical mission.

Friedrich Schleiermacher acknowledged that Christian theology must apply itself to a double task, the cleansing of the church and the spreading of the gospel.   The church always stands in need of being reformed (*ecclesia semper reformanda*) by the word which created it in the first place.   This is the cleansing function of theology.   But the reformation of the church occurs for the sake of its inherent obligation to preach the word by which it lives (*viva vox evangelii*) to all the nations.   This is the propagating function of the church for which theology must prepare the way in every new and different situation.

In recent times Paul Tillich constructed his entire systematic theology as a correlation of two poles of concern, the truth of the Christian message and its interpretation for every new generation.   Theology is kerygmatic when it declares the truth of the message and apologetic when it speaks to the situation of today.   Wolfhart Pannenberg defines the task of theology in light of contemporary hermeneutical theory, particularly Gadamer's, as the fusion of two horizons.   The horizon of the biblical text and the horizon of the present situation must be fused in a new comprehensive horizon shaped by the future of both.   Tillich and Pannenberg both interpret the biblical message in connection with the present situation.   The present situation, however, is not merely the modern world as such and all that exists within it.   The world, biblically understood, is never in a neutral situation.   It is always the "fallen" world that we meet.   In light of the gospel the present situation becomes a missionary situation and the modern world a mission field.

The double task of theology has also been clearly recognized by Jürgen Moltmann.   In *The Crucified God* Moltmann speaks of a double crisis that confronts the church and its theology today: the crisis of relevance and the crisis of identity.   He also describes this double crisis as the identity-involvement dilemma.   For Moltmann the crucified Christ is the principle of Christian identity, and solidarity with the poor and the oppressed is the principle of relevance.   Thus, whether in terms of Schleiermacher's cleansing (*reinigendes*) and propagating (*verbreitendes*) functions of theology, or Tillich's kerygmatic and apologetic aspects, or Pannenberg's hermeneutic fusion of two horizons, or Moltmann's double crisis of identity and relevance, theology always moves in a dialectical tension between the pole of identifying what is specifically Christian and the pole of integrating the common world of human experience into the Christian reality.

A theology of the gospel without the reflex action of missionary praxis easily degenerates into a sterile system of "true doctrines" on which endless theological controversies may take place. The seventeenth century, the heyday of Protestant Orthodoxy, is a case in point. The fury of theologians scoured the church of all false doctrine but did nothing to enflame its zeal for mission. The church of "pure doctrine" was notoriously a church without mission, and its theology therefore more scholastic than apostolic. When replayed on the mission fields many of our traditional dogmatic controversies have proved more effective in making Christians act like heathen than in leading unbelievers to the knowledge of truth.

The combination of a theology of the gospel with the praxis of mission means that theology is not a science which aims to deal with knowledge for its own sake. Schleiermacher revived an earlier definition of theology as a *scientia ad praxin*. This notion is born from the realization that the original matrix of Christian theology is the missionary church. Martin Kähler coined the right expression for it: mission is the mother of theology.[10] In present-day theology Ernst Käsemann has spoken of the origins of theology from another angle when he says: "Apocalyptic was the mother of Christian theology."[11] In the post-Easter situation the earliest theologizing of the primitive Christian mission had its origin in the apocalyptic theology of history. But it was the mission which prevented this apocalypticism from detaching the primitive Christian community from world history, thus averting the fate that befell many a Qumran-like sect of late antiquity. It was no doubt also the missionary situation that prompted the early church to represent the gospel in the Gospels as the history of the crucified and risen Lord. The more the church went forward in mission the more urgent it became to anchor the Word and the Spirit in the history of the Gospels, lest it be carried away by enthusiasm. The missionary proclamation about Jesus Christ became rooted in the soil of Jesus' own preaching of the good news of the kingdom of God. The lesson for theology today is that it must rediscover its beginnings in the missionary situation where the gospel connects up with the traffic of world history. Without the gospel the church and theology have no root; without the mission they bear no fruit.

But if theology needs mission to make it work on the frontline of history, the mission needs the hermeneutical resources of theology to keep it in touch with the home base of the gospel. The modern missionary movement has for the last century and a half been one of the most powerful forces shaping world civilization. Yet most of our biblical and dogmatic theologies have been written within the limited horizon of European and American experience. There has been a divorce of long standing between theology and mission. Theology has turned in upon the church, solving riddles of the past, whereas mission has gropingly reached out to the world with an impact on its future. The divorce goes back to the origins of the evangelical missionary movement in Pietism. Here the highest priority was placed on faith as feeling, on disciplined life rather than correct doctrine, on the individual and his subjective experience rather than the organized church and its affairs, and on the primacy of praxis instead of theory. Orthodoxy had no heart for mission and the Enlightenment could not square it with reason, so it was left to Pietism to assume a near monopoly on the propagating of the faith. Consequently, all the strengths and weaknesses of Pietism have accompanied the missionary movement.

Mission has often been the private interest of pious Christians rather than the foreign policy of the church itself. Its theology has frequently been a mixture of biblical devotion and pious emotion without benefit of the critical historical and constructive achievements of theological scholarship. Church and mission signaled their reconciliation in principle at New Delhi in 1961 when the International Missionary Council merged with the World Council of Churches. It is equally important now that theology and mission regard each other as mutually indispensible, so that the data of the church's missionary encounters in the world shape the themes of theological reflection, and the critical methods of theology clarify the basis and content of the church's missionary faith.

THE NON-MISSIONARY ORIGINS OF PROTESTANTISM

The problem of a Protestant theology of mission is that its classical sources, the theology of the Reformers and the confessional writings, are totally devoid of any missionary consciousness.   Ironically, the Lutheran and Reformed theologians of today who wish to remain loyal to the theology of the sixteenth and seventeenth centuries, of Luther or Calvin and their orthodox followers, must do so in violation of their own Scripture principle *(sola scriptura)*.   The Acts of the Apostles is a history of the earliest Christian missions.   Christianity entered upon the stage of world history as a missionary faith, responding in obedience to the command of the risen Lord: "Go into all the world and preach the gospel to all the nations" (Mark 16:16; see also Matt. 28:18–20; Luke 24:46–48; John 20:21; Acts 1:8; 9:15; 22:21; 26:16–18).   Matthew connects this preaching with the orientation to the end of history: "And this gospel of the kingdom will be preached throughout the whole world, as a testimony to all nations; and then the end will come" (Matt. 24:14).   Every Christian is the product of that missionary history which went forth from Jerusalem, all Judea and Samaria and to the end of the earth (Acts 1:8).   Yet, in the age of Luther and the Reformation the common theological opinion was that the Great Commission had been fulfilled.   Luther said, "No one has any longer such a universal apostolic command, but each bishop or pastor has his appointed diocese or parish."[12]   The Protestant Reformation was, as the term suggests, a confessing movement within the sphere of Christendom.   Reasons can be cited for its lack of missionary activity—the need to establish itself, the lack of contacts with non-Christian people in Protestant lands, involvement in religious wars, opposition to the papacy and monasticism and their kind of missions.   But the fact remains that we search in vain for a theology of mission that permanently obligates the church to preach the gospel of the kingdom throughout the whole world.   Not that Luther and his fellow reformers denied the universality of the gospel. They simply sensed no present need to express it, because the mission to all the nations had already been accomplished on a worldwide scale in the age of the apostles.   The church of today has only to preach the word and administer the sacraments where it is already established.

Luther's eschatology did nothing to drive the church in mission beyond the boundaries of Christendom. The Turks and the Jews and the heathen out there were enemies of the gospel and under the power of the Devil. Besides, Luther was persuaded, along with Melanchthon, that the end of the world was coming soon, sometime in the sixteenth century, so there would hardly be time for the church to mount much of a missionary campaign. Leave it to God! He will save the elect in any case. Here we have a split eschatology, reduplicating in eternity the split between the church and the world in history.

The anti-missionary bent of the Reformation carried over into the age of Protestant Orthodoxy. However, in this period there was not only an absence of missionary ideas, but outright hostility heaped on those who dared to raise their voices. Since missionary interest had emerged among the Anabaptists, that interest suffered from guilt by association. The Anabaptists had carried Luther's principle of the universal priesthood of all believers to the extreme by making the missionary command of our Lord binding on every Christian. The Orthodox response was drawn up by the great dogmatician, Johann Gerhard, who elevated the church's lack of mission to the rank of dogmatic truth. The universality of the missionary command was achieved by the apostles and ceased to be valid thereafter. Somehow the apostles had managed to preach the gospel even in America!

The rise of mission theology in Protestantism begins virtually with the missionary breakthrough in Pietism. But Pietism did not change the theology of Orthodoxy in any basic way. It lifted the Orthodox ban on mission and put into practice the missionary ideas that were "in the air" at that time. Already in the seventeenth century a lone voice crying in the wilderness of Orthodoxy, that of Baron Justinian von Welz, made a passionate plea for the extension of the gospel to the non-Christian world.[13] For him a living faith in the gospel meant to share the love of Christ with the whole world, not least with those who have never heard. Although his Orthodox contemporaries were fiercely unsympathetic, the seeds he sowed became the harvest of mission in the era of Pietism, in a line from Philip Spener and August Herman Francke to Count von Zinzendorf and the Moravian Brethren. This is also the spiritual lineage of Friedrich Schleiermacher, really the first theologian to integrate the study of mission into the theological curriculum.[14] In his *Brief*

Outline on the Study of Theology Schleiermacher states that "the theory of missions . . . is as good as completely lacking up to the present time."[15] The prolific missionary activity in Pietism was largely a case of praxis preceding theory.

Not until the middle of the nineteenth century were serious efforts made to make room in theology for the study of missions. It became classified as one of the subjects of practical theology, giving the impression that mission is not a theological problem but merely a matter of "how to do it." The dogmatic tradition stemming from the period of Orthodoxy was slow to acknowledge the right of mission to become one of the *loci* (topics) of theology. The pietistic tradition was content to *do* mission, without calling for any fundamental changes in the teaching of theology. Missionary circles were mostly content to leave theology alone, neither challenging it nor being corrected by it.

THE ENLIGHTENMENT'S CRITIQUE OF MISSION

As sources, then, for a contemporary theology of mission much of the Protestant tradition is a desert with an oasis here and there. From the Reformation through Orthodoxy to Pietism there is no great reservoir of theology relevant to the worldwide mission of the church. A new challenge arose from an entirely different quarter, the rational theology of the Enlightenment. Two things were to happen before Protestant theology opened up to new sources for the construction of a theology of mission liberated from its defective origins in the Reformation and Orthodoxy. The first was the rise of the historical-critical method. This method made it possible to listen to the Bible in a critical way, with power to challenge the "pure doctrine" of the dogmaticians who had locked out the missionary concern. The second was the rise of the empirical study of world religions. This movement added an abundance of new data about the phenomenon of religion, calling for a revision of the traditional estimate of the relation between Christianity and the non-Christian religions. The Enlightenment was the sponsor of both these novel and creative developments in Protestantism.

One of the precursors of the spirit of the Enlightenment at the time of the Reformation, Erasmus of Rotterdam, had already issued a warm appeal for missionary work, but it found no ready response among

Protestants. The thread of interest was picked up again later by another forerunner of the Enlightenment, Gottfried Wilhelm Leibniz, who was impressed by the Jesuit work in China. Leibniz was apparently not moved so much by evangelical and doctrinal motives toward a world-encompassing mission, but rather by its humanitarian and cultural aspects. When the floodgates of the Enlightenment finally broke and swamped the intellectual circles of Europe, there was no stopping its influence also on the theology and mission of Christianity in relation to the world of culture and religion.

It is customary to credit Pietism with the origins of the modern missionary movement. That is correct, but our theology of mission today owes perhaps as much to the spirit of the Enlightenment. In evangelical circles the Enlightenment is pictured in the worst possible light. A fair-minded account, however, of the sources of many of the ideas which even the evangelicals of today take for granted would end by tracing them straight back to the Enlightenment. Perhaps we can agree with Richard Rothe of the last century who said, "The Enlightenment may have had an awful theology, but not such a bad religion."[16] Not the Reformation, not Luther and Calvin, but the Enlightenment thinkers pleaded for religious tolerance, the right of each individual to enjoy his own religious convictions and to express them freely without political or ecclesiastical harassment. The Enlightenment criticized the use of coercion as a missionary method and recommended instead an appeal to reason and experience without relying on dogmatic or institutional authoritarianism. Few of us would wish to go back on these ideas.

If Pietism deepened the idea of mission to deal with sin as the profoundest human problem separating man from God, it also narrowed down salvation in two respects: it was individualistic and otherworldly. In the Enlightenment the idea of salvation was broadened, at the risk of becoming superficial. Salvation meant emancipation from religious superstition, concern for human welfare, and the moral betterment of mankind. While these interests in human welfare and happiness are surely to be included in the total gospel, they were combined with a one-sidedly optimistic view of the human condition. Sin was understood in moralistic terms. The idea of redemption was reduced to the moral education of the human race. The Enlightenment suffered from the illusion that there was one natural religion underlying all the different religions of the world, including Christianity. The essence of Christianity, like the essence of religion in general, was seen in its moral content. Hence, there is no fundamental difference between Christianity and the other high religions of the world.

The abiding significance of the Enlightenment lies in having reopened the question of the relation between Christianity and the non-Christian religions. Such a question is, of course, nearly as old as Christianity. The early apologists, especially Justin Martyr and Clement of Alexandria, used the famous Greek idea of a *logos spermatikos* to explain a universal revelation of God in all the religions of mankind. But when Christianity became the established religion of the Empire, the other religions were consigned to outer darkness. Augustine could teach that pagan virtues are but "splendid vices." Thomas Aquinas formulated the position of the Catholic Church, integrating the Stoic idea of the logos into a theory of two levels: pagans are on the level of a natural knowledge of God through reason, whereas Christians possess a supernatural knowledge through revelation. Luther and the Reformation generally returned to Augustine's pessimism. With his radical view of human bondage to sin and the devil, Luther could hardly grant to reason any capacity for a true knowledge of God, let alone a saving knowledge apart from Jesus Christ. Only Christianity had such knowledge. Orthodoxy and Pietism also believed that Christianity was the only saving religion. Only with the Enlightenment did there arise a new attitude toward the non-Christian religions. As people became better acquainted with other religions, it became morally impossible to accept the harsh belief that the great masses of humankind outside the sphere of Christianity would be excluded from salvation and damned to eternal hell.

The Enlightenment is to be praised more for the questions it raised than the answers it gave. The question of the relation between Christianity and the rest of the religions was answered by a general disregard for history. The idea that there is an essence of religion inherent in all the positive religions of the world was a rationalistic notion which could arise, as Nathan Söderblom once remarked, only because scholars did not yet possess concrete knowledge of the pagan religions. The Enlightenment thinkers regarded everything historical as accidental and therefore irrelevant. The concrete historical manifestations of a religion are of less importance than that universal essence common to all the religions. It follows from this that the historical revelation of Christianity became viewed as the outer shell of a core of natural religion.

The relevance of the Enlightenment for a theology of mission reached its classical expression in the thinking of Gotthold Ephraim Lessing. His famous fable of the three rings in *Nathan the Wise*, whatever its intention, had the effect of teaching a complete relativism of the religions. Each religion thinks of itself as the true religion, but there is no way to judge for a "thousand thousand years." So the only practical thing is to go on believing that the ring each one—Christianity, Judaism, and Islam—had received from the father is the genuine one. What is the value of the Christian revelation for others? It is pedagogical: it works for the education of humanity, speeding up the time when the truths of revelation in myth and history can be translated into eternal truths of reason. In principle, there is nothing stored up in revelation that human reason, left to itself, cannot attain. Christian mission becomes at best an auxiliary of enlightenment and the development of human culture.

The Enlightenment only dimly recognized the significance of the motif of history in the interpretation of religion. The man who took up this theme and partly overcame the rationalistic moralism of the Enlightenment was Johann Gottfried Herder. It was this category of history that led theology beyond the Enlightenment toward the discovery of history as fundamental to biblical revelation as well as to the nature of man and the relations between cultures and religions. Herder discovered that the essence of being human and of religion itself lies in their individual quality and historical particularity. Everything is tied to history— language and events, knowledge and experience, God and revelation— for nothing that is truly human lies outside the course of history. The religious man too stands within history and nowhere else.

The concept of history might have offered the potential for a totally new theology of mission, serving as the point of departure for a new interpretation of the kingdom of God, and thus forming a bridge between the gospel and the modern world. The relevance of such an eschatological interpretation of history for a theology of the religions might have set the Christian mission on a new footing. But Herder was still standing too much on the ground of the Enlightenment to capitalize on his own idea of history. With respect to the church's mission, Herder believed that each nation, possessing its own culture, language, and religion, stood in no particular need of Christianity. What is a poor Laplander to do with Christian ideas which he cannot understand and which do not belong to his way of life?[17] Anticipating a common trend of today, Herder laid upon Christianity the task of helping and ennobling the other religions, not to convince them of the truth of the Christian faith or to convert them to Christianity. In these ideas Herder did not break away from the Enlightenment or rise above its level of interpreting the mission of the gospel in the world.

THE SYSTEMATIC PLACE OF MISSION IN MODERN THEOLOGY

The nineteenth century was the "Great Century" of Christian missionary outreach, to use Kenneth Scott Latourette's phrase. It was also the century when mission, having come in through the back door, was finally given a decent room in the mansions of systematic theology. As we have shown, the standard theology of the Protestant churches had no locus for mission. In the nineteenth century the sheer volume and success of missionary activity made the subject unavoidable and each school put its own theological stamp on the face of the Christian mission. Most of the ideas that keep cropping up in twentieth-century discussions—systematic, ecumenical, and missiological—can be seen in their embryonic stage of development in the various trends of nineteenth-century theology.

Once in discussing the work of American historians, John K. Fairbank referred to the missionary as "the invisible man of American history."[18] Such is surely the case for historians who write about modern Protestant theology. The impact of the missionary expansion of Christianity on the development of theology is seldom noticed in the histories of Protestant theology. The connections between theology and philosophy have been carefully examined. The results of natural science and biblical criticism and their effects on systematic theology have been accounted for to the last detail. Theology often appears to be a matter of developing scientific ideas about religion in an academic setting, rather than as that which provides the church with a challenging and critical theory of world mission. The man whom Karl Barth called the "father of modern Protestant theology," Friedrich Schleiermacher, was the first to introduce the topic of mission into the theological curriculum. He caught something of Zinzendorf's vision of one world in Christ through his education in the Moravian schools. Schleiermacher's plan for the reorganization of theological studies acknowledges the need to link the science of theology to the praxis of mission. In his *Brief Outline on the Study of Theology* Schleiermacher brought theology into the most intimate connection with the life and mission of the church. The *raison d'être* of theology is to serve the inner life of the church and its work in the world. Schleiermacher confessed in his *Brief Outline* that "the theory of missions . . . is as good as completely lacking up to the present time."[19]

Schleiermacher's contribution to a theology of mission was not limited to finding a place for it in the theological curriculum. In three areas Schleiermacher's theology exercised an enormous influence on the idea of mission in the nineteenth century. First of all, Schleiermacher's *Speeches on Religion* made a convincing case for the notion that the religious dimension is fundamental to the essence of being human. He broke with the Enlightenment's rationalistic idea of a universal essence of religion underlying all the positive religions of the world. Each religion has to be taken as a whole and studied on its own terms. It must not be reduced to some abstract metaphysical or moral principles of which the religious symbols and rites provide only the outer covering. Second, Schleiermacher's thinking advanced considerably from his early *Speeches on Religion* to his later work on dogmatics, *The Christian Faith*, with respect to a theology of the Christian mission. In the *Speeches* there is such a high regard for "feeling" as the locus of all true religion that the positive contents of Christian faith are placed on the same level with all others. Indifference became the price of tolerance. In *The Christian Faith*, however, Schleiermacher establishes a christological basis for the church's encounter with other world religions. "Redemption is posited as a thing which has been universally and completely accomplished by Jesus of Nazareth. . . . Only through Jesus, and thus only in Christianity, has redemption become the central point of religion."[20]   Third, in addition to his christocentric emphasis Schleiermacher places the obligation of mission at the center of the church's existence. Mission is a function of the whole church, not to be kept as a special province of the mission societies.

Schleiermacher's theory of missionary expansion proved defective, however, because he could only support "missions according to the law of continuity." That is to say, the spread of Christianity should take place more like a cultural phenomenon from Christian countries to non-Christian lands adjacent to them. Mission as an apostolic function of the church on a global scale and as a call for individual personal decision on the model of primitive Christianity was not satisfactorily dealt with by Schleiermacher. It is noteworthy that he worked out his complete theory of mission under Christian ethics (*Christliche Sitte*), and thus lost the urgency and finality for mission that in the New Testament emanate from the gospel of eschatological salvation.

A remarkable progression can thus be seen in Schleiermacher's thought. His theology of religion in the *Speeches* leaves no room for the Christian mission. But as a theologian of the church in his later works, *Practical Theology* and *Christian Ethics*, the mission of the church, though limited, takes root both in the theological curriculum and in the system of Christian doctrine. The reason for this change is perhaps the force of the missionary movement itself. Mission was nearly dead at the beginning of the century; it was hardly a lively theme in any of the theologies. Then a renewal movement swept through Christianity, and with it the missionary idea was born again. This gave rise to its own kind of theology, biblical in substance and pietistic in style. August Tholuck, the most prominent theologian of the revival movement, could speak of dogmatics as a scientific summary of biblical faith.

Tholuck and other theologians of the neo-pietistic theology of revivalism retained Schleiermacher's emphasis on subjective feeling in religion. Faith is a matter of free personal decision. Schleiermacher himself had required that a dogmatician have a personal experience of the redemption he is talking about. The pietists strengthened this motif and made personal conversion the precondition of doing real theology. This experience is the criterion and not some abstract canon of secular science. Although this restriction tended to place theology on an island by itself and to isolate Christianity from the world of science and culture, Neo-Pietism in the nineteenth century was at the same time linked to a power source which generated tremendous energy for missionary activity. What was this source of power? Here the theology of revivalism went beyond Schleiermacher's notion of religion as feeling by stressing the objective realities of Scripture which nourished subjective piety. It was not religious feeling as such which drove missionaries to leave home for strange places across the waters. Rather, it was a type of religious experience normed by the objective ground and content of faith in biblical revelation. The pietistic subjectivism that resulted in mission was coupled to a simple, perhaps even literal, attachment to the objective facts of the Bible. The more this revivalist theology of mission revolved around the biblical pole of Christian identity, the more it stressed a wide gulf between Christian faith and pagan religion. Yet, the love of God in Jesus Christ was deemed to be valid also for the heathen and that love provided the main motive of mission for Neo-Pietism.

The history of nineteenth-century Protestant theology usually draws attention to the great theologians—Schleiermacher, Hegel, Rothe, and Ritschl—who attempted to relate Christian faith to the modern mind. They produced a creative synthesis of Christianity with philosophy, science, morality, and culture. To that extent this movement represented the quest of theology for contemporary relevance. Its theology was centrifugal. However, a more complete history of Christianity in the modern world would have to give due credit to the centripetal movement of Pietism which stressed the uniqueness of Christianity and its utter difference from the pagan world. There is irony in the fact that this diastatic theology of Neo-Pietism did as much to shape the face of the modern world through its world mission programs as the theology of synthesis whose chief aim was to adjust the thought forms of Christianity to contemporary culture.

One of the main lines in nineteenth-century theology bears the stamp of Hegel's influence. This was a polar opposite from the mission theology of Pietism.   Schleiermacher's influence, at least in part, could be assimilated by the revivalist theology of the pietistic biblicists because both parties made religious experience the starting point of theological study.   The Hegelian line moved in a different direction, with markedly different results for the theology of mission.   Men such as Rothe, Pfleiderer, Lipsius, and Biedermann attempted to create a synthesis of Christianity with the environing culture.[21]   On the missionary front where Christianity encountered the non-Christian religions, the sharp black-and-white distinctions which Pietism saw between Christianity and heathenism were modified.   Christianity stood with all other religions at some point on an immanental line of religious development from primitive times to the present day.

The danger in this position was that in relativizing the uniqueness of Christianity the missionary idea was close to being abandoned altogether.   But that did not happen.   Christianity was justified in carrying out a mission to culture with other religions because it stands at the highest point in the evolution of humanity.   The motive of mission is the desire to help other religions attain the same level as Christianity. What a difference from Pietism!   The aim of mission is no longer to confront individuals with the preaching of Christ for repentance and faith with a view to eternal salvation, but rather to spread Christian culture, morality, and religion to other people as a whole, and thus to raise them to a higher point of development.   Here in the nineteenth century we see the eruption of a basic and controversial theme in mission theology that prevails to the present day in the contrast between the evangelical line of mission that goes back to Pietism and the ecumenical line that retains continuity with cultural Protestantism.

There were other voices in the nineteenth century which either ignored the theme of mission or were decidedly opposed.   We have already called attention to the position of Protestant Orthodoxy.   The missionary command of our Lord was supposedly already fulfilled by the apostles in the first century, and thus no longer binding today.   One of the most famous biblicist theologians of the nineteenth century renewed the proposition of seventeenth century Orthodoxy.   He was J. T. Beck of Tübingen.[22]   But his reasoning was different.   According to New Testament eschatology, Christ will return and when he does, he will convert the heathen and establish his kingdom. The mission of the church has nothing to do with it, as the mission societies of his day imagined. Christians ought to serve their own people. That is enough. The nations of the world will be converted to Christ in some future period of the kingdom of God, but the signs of the times are not ripe for it now.

Another theologian of great reknown who, although writing voluminously on almost every subject of theology, had nothing positive to say about the Christian world mission was Albrecht Ritschl. One can only speculate that this blind spot was caused, perhaps, by his great antipathy to Pietism which had made mission its specialty. Can anything good come out of Pietism? Not for Ritschl. On this point he was a poor judge. On the other side, however, it can be acknowledged that Ritschl's leading idea of the kingdom of God offered a congenial starting point for constructing a theology of the Christian mission of universal relevance. However, Ritschl's theology was unable to free itself, here as in most other respects, from the narrow horizon of his own bourgeois cultural setting.

The nineteenth century is climaxed by a clear juxtaposition of the two types of theology of mission we have briefly sketched. This is clearly evident in the contrast between Martin Kähler and Ernst Troeltsch. They are vigorous advocates of two different ways of thinking about mission, both standing on the threshold of the Barthian revolution in theology. As the story is frequently told one gets the impression that theology had completely fallen prey to the cultural syntheses of Neo-Protestantism, making the entire nineteenth century a colossal betrayal of biblical Christianity. Such an estimate is now more easily recognized as a misreading of the nineteenth century. It was born of an excessive enthusiasm among the youthful leaders of Neo-Orthodoxy—Karl Barth and Emil Brunner. Martin Kähler and Ernst Troeltsch, for example, are too important for a theology of mission today to be covered over by an avalanche of negative criticism. A brief comparison of their typical differences can help us to see the deeper roots of problems that still remain unsolved.

Martin Kähler was the first of the theologians to give a distinct place to the idea of mission in his systematic theology.[23]   Others like Ritschl had not even mentioned it.   For Kähler mission belonged to the essence of Christianity, and was not only one of its chance historical manifestations.   The preaching of Christianity is rooted in the gospel.   This is the suprahistorical word of God which as such occurs in history without being reducible to it.   No limits can be placed on the gospel.   It is universally valid.   The mission it generates is clearly to be distinguished from propaganda, because it occurs in the consciousness of a divine commission.   Kähler believed it presumptuous to argue for a Christian mission on the ground of historical relativism.   The decisive question is whether Christianity points to a suprahistorical message valid for every religion, something which can truly be called the "word of God."   On a purely human plane what right do Christians have to claim any religious superiority over others?

For Kähler the motive of mission was to share the message of redemption.   Redemption in the biblical sense is something else than cultural development to a higher plane.   The gospel is the gift of salvation, not a goad to moral elevation.   The evangelical core of the pietistic concern for mission was accentuated by Kähler.   There is little justification for Christianity to enter the battle of the religions unless it has a message of eternal value that comes from God and bears on the salvation of all people.   Otherwise the Christian mission becomes cultural propaganda and religious imperialism.   Kähler's contribution to a theology of mission was to purge it of its secondary cultural accretions. He articulated the spirit and vision of the first apostles whose sole reason for mission was the word and command of the Lord.   Kähler brought relentless criticism to bear on the competing notion of mission which reached its zenith in the thought of Ernst Troeltsch.

If we can view Kähler's thought as the precursor of the Barthian theology of mission, we can with equal justification view Ernst Troeltsch's point of view as the outcome of the evolutionary-historical line that began in German idealism.   Troeltsch was the systematic theologian of the History-of-Religions School.[24]   He advocated a new view of Christianity, one which would leave aside all dogmatism, supernaturalism, absolutism, and exclusivism.   All religions, including Christianity, were to be studied from a strictly historical point of view.   The results brought not only a new assessment of the biblical origins of Christianity, but also a new systematic concept of the relation between Christianity and the other religions and of the way in which God works through all of them.

For Troeltsch, in contrast to Kähler, God's revelation in the Bible and through Jesus Christ represents only one stage in the universal history of God's revelation in the religions.   There can be no absolute religion in the midst of the relativities of history.   The Absolute lies at the end of history, and only then can a final judgment on the religions be made. But even now it is possible to make some distinctions on historical grounds.   Christianity does not represent a category different from other religions, but it does show itself to be relatively higher through its historical success, spiritual power, and rationality.   Christianity enjoys a superior participation in the Absolute which to a lesser degree shines through other religions as well.   Here we have a slender thread on which to hang the Christian mission in world history.

The essence of the Christian mission for Troeltsch does not lie in bringing the gospel of salvation to the pagan world.   Every religion is on a road toward the Absolute in a way appropriate to its own cultural situation.   The most we can expect is a cross-fertilization of religious ideas in which Christianity might play the role of raising other religions to a greater fulfillment of their own potential.   The aim of mission is not conversion but only a development to higher religious sophistication. For Troeltsch, Protestant that he was in the Idealist tradition, the highest form of religious experience to be attained is an individual personal relation to God.   Neither Christian dogma nor church institution holds any real importance in giving birth to such an experience.   Not even the person of Jesus Christ as the center of faith is of permanent validity in the relationship of the individual to God.   What is of lasting importance is the principle of Christianity which transcends Christianity itself as well as every other concrete confession of faith.   Mission according to this principle—something other than the gospel in Kähler's sense—will lead to contact and dialogue with other religions.   But in the end Christianity is viewed as the religion of Europe and America, not as a faith with universal validity for all the world.

ESCHATOLOGY AND MISSION IN
CONTEMPORARY THEOLOGY

Ernest Troeltsch said at the end of the nineteenth century: "The bureau of eschatology is mostly closed nowadays."[25] At about the same time Albert Schweitzer found eschatology to be the key to the message of Jesus. This opened up a new chapter in theology. No history of twentieth-century theology could be written without taking into account the variant meanings of eschatology. The diversity runs the gamut from Karl Barth to Rudolf Bultmann and from Wolfhart Pannenberg to Gustavo Gutierrez. It is not surprising then that eschatology has placed its stamp on the theology of mission that comes out of the twentieth century.

At first the impact of Karl Barth's transcendental eschatology had a negative effect on the theology of mission. Eschatology became a tool of a negative dialectic in which the radical otherness of God confronted the church and called it into question. The missions of the Western churches appeared all too secular. Missionaries were getting into the business of education, medicine, and even cultural and political activities. Missionaries could be seen as leading agents of Western secularism spreading from Europe and America throughout Africa and Asia, when they were properly called and sent to preach the word of God and nothing else. It appeared that Barthian theology would have nothing but judgment to pronounce on the mission of the church.

Karl Barth, however, spoke at a mission conference in 1932 on the theme, "Theology and Mission Today."[26] Here we have the clearest expression of the relation between dialectical eschatology and mission. Barth squelched the suspicion that his theology of crisis implied a total rejection of the missionary enterprise. There is a crisis in mission, to be sure, but theology must wrestle with mission like the angel with Jacob.

Barth defines mission as the work of the church proclaiming the word of God to those who have not heard. Since all who have heard are still sinners, however, the word must be addressed to them as well. So there is only one mission, one ministry of the word of God—to all. The motive of mission has been variously expressed. Some say it lies in the nature of faith to share what it has, others that it belongs to the essence of the gospel to be addressed to all people, and still others that the need of the world cries out for help. All these are true, Barth says, but they do not reach far enough. The deepest motive, the one on which all the others depend, is simply the command of the Lord. Without the clear backing of the sovereign will of the Lord there is no certainty of the validity of the other motives.

On the task of mission, Barth lays all stress on faithful witness to the word of God. The pietists aimed at the conversion of souls; the Anglo-American approach was intent on spreading Christian civilization; and a Lutheran view which operated under the doctrine of the orders of creation tried to bring each ethnic group to its own providential fulfillment. Again, Barth says, none of these can stand by itself; all are secondary to the main task of unswerving witness to the word of God. The word is free to be concretely related to each and every situation. But it must always remain the master and not be taken captive to some law of indigenous culture. Barth issued a warning against the danger of making the word of God the slave of a particular culture, whether European, American, African, or Asian. No culture can be normative. The only acceptable normative form of the word of God in history is the written word of God—the Bible. There is no immanent point of contact—*Anknüpfungspunkt*—in human language or culture, in morality or religion. There is no latent potentiality from below for the true word of God. From the human side there is sheer discontinuity. The contact of the word of God and human culture is an event that occurs by grace alone and is always a miracle.

The *leitmotiv* in Barth's theology of mission is that there is only one foundation of mission, namely, the biblical revelation of God in Christ. Here alone we have the witness to eschatological revelation and the word of eschatological salvation. There is no prior anthropological foundation of mission, no line of preparation for the revelation of God in the history of religion. The only revelation, the only salvation, is that which comes vertically from above. Its only medium is Jesus Christ.

Barth's exclusive christocentric concept of saving revelation made its entry into mission circles by way of Hendrik Kraemer's famous book, *The Christian Message in a Non-Christian World.*[27] Kraemer emphasized the radical lostness of man on his own. All the religions of the world, in light of biblical realism, are seen as products of the self-assertive pride of man over against the one true God, the Father of Abraham, Isaac, and Jacob. They all fall under the judgment of God. There is no point of contact in these religions, for they are all penetrated by the pride of man. Even the empirical church stands under this same divine judgment. In this ultimate respect Christianity is in no better position than all the non-Christian religions. The only difference between the church and the world religions is that the church knows it stands under the judgment of God and has heard the gracious verdict of God's justification in Christ.

The name of Rudolf Bultmann is not customarily associated with the mission of the church. Yet, he ranks second only to Karl Barth as the most influential Protestant theologian of the twentieth century. Along with terms like *kerygma* and *existence* he lifted the word *eschatology* into the common vocabulary of every neophyte theologian. For Bultmann the word *eschatology* means "ultimate and final salvation in its existential concreteness—in personal decision, faith, and obedience." Eschatology does not have to do with future events in history; rather, it has to do with every moment of existence so far as it is a matter of existential decision.

What bearing does such an eschatology have on the mission of the church? Bultmann has never answered such a question in terms of a theology of mission. However, Bultmann's ideas have made a positive contribution to the attempt to consider the nature of mission in the light of eschatology. One of Bultmann's disciples, Walter Holsten, has drawn out the missionary implications of Bultmann's theology. In an essay entitled, "Mission as Eschatological Event,"[28] Holsten states that the mission must not be understood as a *means* to the eschaton, but as the effect of the eschaton. Mission and eschatology are related not as means to end, but as effect and cause. The eschaton from which mission proceeds is the justifying act of God in Jesus Christ; the mission is a reactualization of the eschatological event of salvation in every present moment.

The most important tense of eschatological thinking is the present. The eschaton is the saving act of God for each individual in every moment of decision. The Lutheran accent is unmistakable—the justification of the sinner through faith, which occurs through the kerygmatic proclamation of the crucified and risen Christ. The sole subject of mission is the kerygma, the message of God who acts. The sole object of mission is the individual person, not the condition of things in the cultural, political, and social spheres. The sole method of mission is the preaching of the kerygma, not such things as education, medicine, or social welfare. The sole aim of mission is salvation, not the improvement of man's earthly welfare. Not *das Wohl* but *das Heil* is the task of missionary activity.

It is difficult to believe that such a kerygma-centered theology of mission could have been written in the context of any real missionary praxis. Its focus on the conversion of the individual would make little sense in Africa or Asia where the meaning of the individual cannot be abstracted from his relation to the whole community. Its sharp distinction between the visible church as a sociological phenomenon and the invisible church as an eschatological event is vapid to a missionary who is sweating to plant the church in a new land. Its cleavage between the ministry of the historical Jesus and the mission of the kerygmatic Christ today does little to help the evangelist who has to translate the gospel into the idioms of a foreign tongue. All these distinctions and dichotomies are brain waves of a purely academic exercise. They have not emanated from concrete praxis in the field of mission.

Paul Tillich, like Barth and Bultmann, struggled throughout his career to make good the meaning of eschatology. In the 1920s he developed the theory of religious socialism as a way between two pitfalls.[29] On the one side, he sought to overcome the immanentism of modern socialism by lifting up the transcendent symbols of biblical eschatology. On the other side, Tillich was trying to overcome Lutheran orthodoxism, which, on the basis of the static and dichotomous two-kingdoms doctrine, kept its theology of the orders of creation separate from the history of redemption.

The basic proposition of Tillich's theology of mission is that the meaning of history lies in the kingdom of God.[30] The mission of the kingdom of God takes place within the horizon of history. History is the field of struggle between two opposing forces, the one driving toward fulfillment in the kingdom of God, the other toward disruption through the destructive power of the demonic. The symbol of the kingdom of

God points to an unambiguous future of history in which the demonic is conquered, fulfillment is reached, and ambiguity is overcome. With this statement Tillich disavows the utopian notion that the kingdom of God will be reached sometime in the future. As long as life moves forward on the plane of history, the battle will always go on between divine and demonic forces. Tillich's notion is dialectical. There will be a real fulfillment of history brought about through history, but not perfectly realized in history. Somehow the historical process contributes to the transcendent realization of the kingdom of God above and beyond history.

The church is the representative of the kingdom of God in history. Its mission is to fight for the kingdom of God. As the agent of the kingdom the church partially embodies what it anticipates as the eschatological fulfillment of history.

History is divided into two sections, B.C. and A.D. The point between is called the center of history. The center is the New Being in Jesus as the Christ. He is the event in which the meaning of history becomes manifest. Unlike Barth and Kraemer, Tillich believes that there is a preparation going on everywhere for the manifestation of the center in history. The church is latently present in Judaism, in paganism, and even in secular humanism. The church emerges out of its latency and becomes manifest wherever people receive the message of the New Being in Jesus as the Christ.

What then is mission? Mission is the activity of the church by which it works for the transformation of its own latency into its self-manifestation all over the world. There are three inadequate interpretations of mission. First, it is not, as Pietism thinks, an attempt to save as many souls as possible from eternal damnation. Such an idea is defective on several accounts: it presupposes the possibility of separating an individual from the social group of which he is a part, and it is an idea unworthy of the glory and love of God and the inclusiveness of his saving revelation in Jesus Christ. Nor, secondly, is mission, as in nineteenth-century liberalism, simply a cross-fertilization of cultures. Mission is not a function of culture, but of the church. It has to do with planting the church and spreading the faith rather than cultural exchange programs. Another inadequate explanation of mission, finally, is to make it an instrument to unite all world religions. Such a union of religions presupposes a common denominator shared by all. If there were such a thing, that would have to become the center of history and thus displace the centrality of Jesus the Christ. The Christian church would be reduced to one religion among others, and thus lose its role as special agent of the kingdom of God.

The nineteenth century searched for a formula of comparison between Christianity and other religions. It became common to speak of Christianity as the absolute religion. Tillich did not like the phrase "the absoluteness of Christianity." He preferred to speak of "the universality of the Christian message."[31] What is at stake is not the preservation of any particular form of Christianity, but only the claim that Jesus is the Christ, the bringer of the New Being. The one who brings the New Being is an absolute figure with universal meaning, whereas Christianity is always expressed in relative historical forms that live for awhile and then pass away. The greatness of the Christian mission, despite its overwhelming attachment to Western culture, is that it has successfully started new churches in non-Western culture. This is the best proof of the transcendent origins and universal validity of the Christian message.

In Barth, Bultmann, and Tillich we have three ways in which eschatology has defined the meaning of mission in Protestant theology. Barth oriented mission to the transcendent word of God and the church's witness to it, Bultmann to the kerygma and the existential decision of the self, and Tillich to the kingdom of God as the final meaning of history. In the early 1930s Oscar Cullmann offered another approach to New Testament eschatology with the closest possible link to the idea of mission. It is the approach of salvation history (*Heilsgeschichte*).[32]

According to Cullmann the history of salvation has not come to an end with the incarnation, but continues on until the parousia. The central event in the continuation of salvation history is the preaching of the gospel to the nations. This is the meaning of mission. The mission begins with the end that has already arrived in Christ and runs forward to the final end that will be manifest in the parousia. This is similar to Tillich's notion of Christ as the center of history. However, Cullmann's formulation of a theology of mission has exerted a greater influence on Protestant missiology, perhaps on account of its closer adherence to biblical categories and its explicit dependence on primitive Christian eschatology.

First, mission is a preparation for the end.   The line of salvation history which runs from the incarnation and is extended forward by the mission of the church has the purpose of preparing the world for the return of Christ.   According to Cullmann, the end of history will not occur until the preaching of the gospel to all the nations has run its course.   The preaching of the gospel has an inner connection with the coming of the end, for in preaching a person encounters the One who is coming.   He is asked to make a decision for or against Christ.

Cullmann's view places the highest possible premium on the missionary proclamation of the gospel.   It stands as the condition of the arrival of the end.   This does not mean, of course, that the preaching will be successful in the sense that all the nations will be converted.   Far from it!   Only the possibility of conversion, only the actual confrontation with the gospel has been promised.   There is no promise that the church will grow and prosper in history.   Actually, the preaching of the gospel will go against the church.   Much of the church will be found faithless as the time of the end ripens.

Second, mission is a sign of the end.   We may not be able to hasten or delay the coming of the end by the way we preach the gospel.   We may not be able to stand in its path or speed it up.   But wherever real preaching of the gospel is taking place, it is an eschatological event, no matter how long history lasts.   We do not have the means to calculate the hour of the end by looking at the sign.   We can only know from the sign that the end will surely come.

These two ideas stand in tension with each other; the one that the mission of preaching to all the nations must first occur before the end comes, and the other that we can know nothing about the time of the coming, whether sooner or later.   Cullmann does not attempt to resolve the tension.   In this respect he leaves the matter where it lies in the New Testament—systematically unresolved.

Finally, mission is related to the postponement of the parousia.   The question is then whether in intensifying the mission it is possible to fulfill the condition of the end more quickly. This would seem to follow logically, but the New Testament makes clear that the final end can by no means be influenced by our own good or bad deeds. Our actions do not play the determinative role, for the kingdom will come by the initiative of the sovereign will of God and nothing else. We are faced with a dilemma. The mission is an essential condition of the end; it must be fulfilled; we are involved in it. Yet, it is up to God alone. It is not dependent on human will and knowledge, or missionary achievements and success. Cullmann gives an answer in line with the evangelical Reformation of Luther and Calvin. There is true and false preaching. Preaching is true when it confronts people with the kingdom of God, but when that happens, it is God's work and not man's. God himself is at work in history fulfilling the condition on which the coming of the end depends. Thus there is no room for synergism as an explanation of the relation of mission to eschatology. Eschatological salvation reaches the world on the plan of God's grace alone, and not as a product of church planning and mission programs.

What comes through most clearly in Cullmann's idea of mission is its relation to the future eschaton. The biblical symbols that point to the future destiny of the world are intimately connected with the mission of the church. Eschatological symbols offer a new point of departure for a theology of mission and the interpretation of human experience and world history. This idea of the future tense in eschatological thinking as it impinges on mission was pretty much overshadowed by the controlling influence of Barth and Bultmann just before and after World War II. It remained latent until the combined impact of Wolfhart Pannenberg's theology of history and Jürgen Moltmann's theology of hope broke through to a new historical eschatology in which the future holds the primacy. Both emphasized that eschatology without the future of the eschaton is no eschatology at all, but only axiology or mysticism. Both criticized the shift from the category of hope in the oncoming future of God to faith as the experience of his timeless presence. We are still in the midst of the movement to reformulate a theology of mission in light of a futurist eschatology. This book is an attempt to spell out the categories and to draw out some implications for a theology of mission in light of the kingdom of God and the emerging shape of the world today.

NOTES

1. *Re-thinking Missions*, by The Commission of Appraisal, William Ernest Hocking, Chairman (New York: Harper & Brothers, 1932), p. 35.

2. *Ibid.*

3. *Ibid.*

4. *Ibid.*, p. 33.

5. *Ibid.*, p. 44.

6. *Ibid.*, p. 47.

7. John Hick, *God and the Universe of Faiths* (New York: Macmillan, 1973), p. 121.

8. John Hick's proposal will perhaps be applauded by those who welcomed H. R. Niebuhr's declamations against radical christocentrism in theology, which he called "a unitarianism of the Second Article," proposing instead a retrieval of "radical monotheism." I have always felt, to the contrary, that a Christian theologian who looks away from Christ for his doctrine of God is a contradiction in terms. Moltmann's blunt assertion is to the point: "Christianity cannot therefore any longer be represented as a 'monotheistic form of belief' (Schleiermacher). Christian faith is not 'radical monotheism'. As a theology of the cross, Christian theology is the criticism of and liberation from philosophical and political monotheism." Jürgen Moltmann, *The Crucified God* (New York: Harper & Row, 1974), pp. 215–216.

9. Emil Brunner, *The Word and the World* (London: SCM, 1931), p. 108.

10. Martin Kähler, *Die Mission—ist sie ein unentbehrlicher Zug am Christentum? in Schriften zu Christologie und Mission* (Munich: Chr. Kaiser, 1971), p. 190.

11. Ernst Käsemann, "The Beginnings of Christian Theology," *New Testament Questions of Today* (Philadelphia: Fortress, 1969), p. 102.

12. Quoted by Gustav Warneck, *Outline of a History of Protestant Missions* (New York: Fleming H. Revell, 1906), pp. 14–15.

13. Cf. the book of my colleague, James Scherer, *Justinian Welz: Essays by an Early Prophet of Mission* (Grand Rapids, Mich.: Eerdmans, 1969).

14. Olav Guttorm Myklebust, *The Study of Missions in Theological Education* (Oslo: Land og Kirke, 1955), Vol. I, p. 51.

15. Friedrich Schleiermacher, *Brief Outline on the Study of Theology* (Richmond, Virginia: John Knox, 1966), paragraph 298.

16. Quoted by Martin Richter, "Aufklärung und Mission," *Neue Allgemeine Missionszeitschrift*, (Gütersloh: C. Bertelsmann, 1929), p. 7.

17. See Martin Richter, *Der Missionsgedanke im evangelischen Deutschland des 18. Jahrhunderts* (Leipzig: Hinrich, 1928), p. 165, n. 6.

18. John K. Fairbank, "Assignment for the '70s," *American Historical Review* (February, 1969), p. 99.

19. *op. cit.*, paragraph 298.

20. Friedrich Schleiermacher, *The Christian Faith* (Philadelphia: Fortress, 1977), pp. 56, 57.

21. See Ernst zur Nieden, *Der Missionsgedanke in der systematischen Theologie seit Schleiermacher* (Gütersloh: C. Bertelsmann, 1928), pp. 89–103.

22. *Ibid.*, pp. 86–89.

23. The most important of Martin Kähler's writings on mission are: *Der Menschensohn und seine Sendung an die Menschheit; Die Bedeutung der Mission für Leben und Lehre der Kirche; Die Mission—ist sie ein unentbehrlicher Zug am Christentum? Weltversohnung und Weltmission.* These can be found, among others, in a recent edition of Martin Kähler's mission writings, *Schriften zu Christologie und Mission* (Munich: Chr. Kaiser, 1971).

24. See Paul Knitter's discussion of Ernst Troeltsch's theology of the religions in his doctoral dissertation, *Towards a Protestant Theology of the Religions* (Marburg: N. G. Elwert, 1974), pp. 5–20. Knitter's work is informed by Karl Rahner's

viewpoints on "anonymous Christianity" and H. R. Schlette's on the world religions as the ordinary way of salvation.

25. Quoted by Ludwig Wiedenmann, *Mission und Eschatologie* (Paderborn: Bonifacius, 1965), p. 11.

26. Published in a collection of Barth's essays, *Theologische Fragen und Antworten* III (Zürich: Evangelischer Verlag, 1957), pp. 100–126.

27. Hendrik Kraemer, *The Christian Message in a Non-Christian World* (New York, Harper, 1938).

28. Walter Holsten, "Mission als eschatologisches Geschehen," in L. Hennig ed., *Theologie und Liturgie* (Kassel, 1952), pp. 183–196. See also Holsten's book, *Das Kerygma und der Mensch, Einführung in die Religions—und Missionswissenschaft* (Munich, Chr. Kaiser, 1953).

29. See the essays on religious socialism in Paul Tillich, *Political Expectation*, James Luther Adams ed., (New York: Harper & Row, 1971).

30. Paul Tillich, "Missions and World History," in *The Theology of the Christian Mission*, Gerald H. Anderson ed., (New York: McGraw-Hill, 1961), pp. 281–289.

31. *Ibid.*, p. 286.

32. In addition to his most famous work, *Christ and Time* (Philadelphia: Westminster, 1950), Oscar Cullmann addressed the theme of eschatology and mission in a number of essays:

"Le caractère eschatologique du devoir missionnaire et de la conscience apostolique de Saint Paul," in *Revue d'histoire et de philosophie religieuses* (Strasbourg, 1936), 16, 210–245.

"Eschatology and Missions in the New Testament," in *The Background of the New Testament and Its Eschatology*, W. D. Davies and David Daube eds., (Cambridge University Press, 1956), pp. 409–421.

"Quand reviendra le royaume de Dieu?" in *Revue d'histoire et de philosophie religieuses* (Strasbourg, 1938), 18, 174–186.

2

THE KINGDOM OF GOD
IN HISTORY

THE KINGDOM OF GOD AND MISSION

A fruitful point of contact for theology and mission today is the rediscovery of the importance of eschatology. From the side of theology there is widespread recognition of the eschatological dimension of basic Christian concepts, such as revelation, faith, and history. Minus its eschatology the gospel becomes reduced to ethics.[1] From the beginning Christianity entered the world of history as an eschatological faith. Eschatology cannot be isolated from other themes of faith and dealt with in a treatise on "the last things." Instead, it determines the horizon of all Christian understanding and is thematically structural for all the contents of faith and action.

On the side of mission the eschatological vision has been the driving motive of the missionary movement. Eschatology was kept alive in missionary circles when it had virtually died out in the church and the schools of theology. But what kind of eschatology? It was the biblical legacy from Pietism which furnished the missionary movement with its eschatological ideas. These ideas were usually digested raw—literalistically—without benefit of modern cooking. Hence, the meaning of eschatology in missionary circles is often felt to be a totally different species from the animal that goes by the same name in modern theology. Yet both read the same Bible and live in the same world. How can such different things be meant when they share the same hope in the end?

The central idea of biblical eschatology is the message of Jesus, the gospel of the kingdom of God. This would seem the place to begin a theology of mission with roots in the gospel of Jesus Christ. Those who have bad memories of the Social Gospel movement in America and of the Kant-Ritschlian influence on Protestant theology in general will be shy, perhaps even disturbed, about the decision to take "Jesus and the kingdom of God" as the starting point of a theology of the Christian mission.[2] Is this not just a leaf out of the old liberal notebook that registered a deficit for the church and its theology last time they took this route? However that may be, we cannot rewrite the Gospels, and Jesus cannot be blamed for what others have done to his central idea.

In the tradition of the Reformation it has been customary to make the article of justification the starting point of theology. The doctrine of justification, it has been said, is the article by which the church stands or falls (*articulus stantis et cadentis ecclesiae*). This is the gospel according to St. Paul. It is an unfortunate mistake, however, to place Paul's teaching of justification by faith against Jesus' preaching of the kingdom of God. But surely, if it came to a competition the Christian would know where to stand. He would only have to study Paul. Paul never imagined he was setting up his own theology as an alternative to the message of Jesus. The justification of the sinner, in Paul's theology, is the communication of the righteousness of God which for both Jesus and Paul is a predicate of his one kingly rule. No one can enter into the kingdom of God except he come clothed in the robes of a righteousness from above. Justification is the answer to the question of how a person can enter the kingdom of God when he is still a sinner. To seek the kingdom of God and to seek the righteousness which God demands are one and the same quest. They come as a gift from beyond the seeker, not as a result of any merits or particular worthiness. Whoever is justified stands within the chosen circle of those who are called and converted by the Spirit to the kingdom of God.

As far as the objection is concerned that the Social Gospel movement adopted "Jesus and the kingdom of God" as its biblical point of departure, the old rule is perfectly applicable: *abusus non tollit usum*. Between our affirmation of a theology of the kingdom of God and the Social Gospel in America there lie the critiques of the History-of-Religions School, particularly the works of Johannes Weiss and Albert Schweitzer, which spelled the death of the immanental, progressivistic, evolutionary, and ethical concept of the kingdom of God in Protestant liberalism. In the preaching of Jesus the kingdom of God is not an inner-worldly process of development that leads to a better world through ethical striving, social reform, and political activity. The kingdom of God is rather, according to the school of radical eschatology, the power of God's own absolute future breaking in suddenly upon the present world, not the guarantee of continuing the way it is nor the crowning fulfillment of its progress. The kingdom arrives where and when the Spirit wills. It is something for which we can "watch and pray" in a spirit of radical openness. When it comes, it does so on its own terms and not as a result of human calculations and controls. The future eschatological kingdom is theocentric and transcendental, and for just this reason we can look to it with great hope as the infinite source of newness and lasting freedom.

Not only the theology of the Ritschlian School and the social gospel, but also today's process and liberation theologies must be held accountable to the eschatological concept of the kingdom of God in the message of Jesus. Why is this important? Because without it we are too easily deceived into believing that salvation lies in our grasp, at our disposal, something we bring about. The parables of the kingdom tell us neither that eschatological salvation is a subjective state of mind that we can achieve through techniques like Transactional Analysis, Positive Mental Attitude, or Transcendental Meditation, nor that it is an unfolding process of development according to the inherent laws of nature or history. The salvation of the eschatological kingdom is totally God's own work. There is no room here for any kind of Pelagianism which throws the coming of the kingdom into our laps, whether by some new or old Pharisaic observance of the law, some new or old pietistic religious enthusiasm, some new or old zeal for ideological politics. That sounds as though the politics of the kingdom provides a convenient excuse for doing nothing. But neither is there free room for doing nothing, because that too must come under the judgment of the approaching kingdom. There is no sanctuary in quietism, neutrality or ascetic withdrawal from the field of battle. Whether we sit on our hands or risk our necks, we are doing something with our lives and neither is the cornerstone of the new world that God is building.

The implications of this monergistic note are at least threefold: (1) because God is working all in all, no corner of the world is left to the sovereignty of human autonomy. There is no secular sphere which runs on its own. There is one Lord, implying a universal coverage of the human situation; (2) because everything stands under the rule of God, all human grounds for boasting, for practicing apartheid, and for class distinctions have been broken. The rule of God has the force to relativize every human tendency to absolutize a segment of reality, to elevate it to the point of idolatry and use it as an instrument against humanity; (3) because the kingdom of God is totally efficacious, there is solid ground for hope in the midst of the sin, sickness, and suffering of this present age. God's rule has drawn near; in Christ it is already here as the decision of God to take sides with the world, and to make good the universal promise of life for every person and every community, beginning (though not ending) with those at the bottom and on the fringes of life.

The confidence that "if God be for us, who can be against us?" has sustained people in their struggles for freedom when every other support has collapsed and they have nothing on which to stand except to launch out in faith toward the future. The belief that "the kingdom of God comes indeed of itself" and not as the cumulative result of the religious and social good works of people and their systems is not an excuse for doing nothing but the ground of the courage to risk all in faith and freedom, to strike out into the unknown future with great hope and joy.

We conclude, then, that the gospel of the kingdom of God can be taken as the most adequate starting point for the mission of the church. This does not displace the doctrine of justification central to Reformation theology.[3] Instead, justification is interpreted as the answer to the question of how we can exchange our rags for the robes of a righteousness not our own (*extra nos*). Nor does the gospel of the kingdom of God repristinate the ethicization of Christianity in the Social Gospel movement. The priority of the eschatological dimension of the kingdom over the ethical stands between us. However, there are values in the theology of the Social Gospel which can be integrated into an eschatological interpretation of the kingdom of God in world history. For reconceptualizing the mission of the church we would acknowledge two points of permanent significance. First, the Social Gospel pointed out the error of reducing salvation to the individual and his personal relation to God. A person who is saved minus all his relationships to the world of nature, society, and other individuals is a pure abstraction. One Social Gospeller defined Christianity as "the transformation of life upon the earth into a kingdom of righteousness and not merely a means for saving a small remnant of humanity into a state of future bliss."[4] We retain a certain continuity, then, with the theology of the Social Gospel when we emphasize that the kingdom of God bears a relation not only to the individual, but to the widest possible range of life in social, political, and economic structures. Secondly, we stand with the Social Gospel when today we emphasize that the kingdom of God is not merely a religious message that points to a supernatural life beyond this world, but is the power of the ultimate future penetrating the secular life of mankind, making it determinative "on earth as it is in heaven."

The mission of the church is God's bridge to a world which has not yet come home to the place prepared for it. If the kingdom of God would already have arrived in its power and glory on earth, there would be no need for mission. We would be living in the time of universal fulfillment, eternal play, and celebrative rapture. But such is not the case. The gospel is the presence of the kingdom in Jesus under the signs of his words and deeds, with special concentration on the double ending of his life—his cross and resurrection. The mission is the means by which the *future* of the kingdom moves the world toward its final salvation. The structure of world history is thus marked by the presence and the future of the kingdom of God, revealed to us in the ministry of Jesus and the earliest Christian apostolate.

Faith in the gospel is always qualified by hope in the word that promises far more than the world has ever seen. Faith is hope insofar as the gospel is promise. The kingdom of God is both the foundation of the church and the goal of the world. Therefore, we have and we hope; we give thanks and we sigh for more. Living in the tension of such a posture, we cannot be religious dropouts with an idle faith and a passive hope. The call of the kingdom is an invitation to work while it is day, to be active in love, to sow the seeds of the word and spread the flame of the Spirit.

Modern ecumenical history has confirmed the close connection between eschatological faith and missionary action.[5] As the churches searched for a common ground of unity and clarity of witness in the missionary situation, they inevitably had to appeal away from their separate traditions to the Bible. The Bible is always the bad conscience of a church which forgets its eschatology and its propelling missionary impulse. As the churches converge on a common path in the future, they will necessarily rediscover the biblical mediation of that future in the preaching which founded the church and keeps the church restless in mission until the end of history. The ecumenical movement as a mere effort to get the churches together proves to be a tiresome bureaucratic system unless it issues from the eschatological ground of mission. The eschatological horizon of its faith in Christ makes the church a messianic movement in history. The missionary imperative fades away when the churches turn in upon themselves and lose contact with God's eschatological mission to the world. The gospel must be preached to all the nations. That is the meaning of history that runs from the appearance of the Easter Jesus to his final manifestation as the Lord of the cosmos. The missionary drive of the church fits into that scheme; otherwise the church becomes the religious shell of the dying culture of Christendom.

THE EXPERIENTIAL ROOTS OF ESCHATOLOGICAL FAITH

The torch of salvation which the early Christians passed on to the world was aflame with images of the end of the world, the return of Christ, the resurrection of the dead, the final judgment. These and many similar images clustered around the central Christian belief that the power and glory of God's kingdom would be established in the end, and that in fact this end had already occurred beforehand in Jesus Christ.

There was, however, no single eschatological scheme—no one theological model of the future—that answered all possible questions about the what, where, when, and why of the coming kingdom. But this lack of clear conceptuality and coherent symbolism does not mean that one could treat these eschatological ideas as so much husk to be thrown away, holding back a kernel of faith for our time.

Whenever Christianity has been found ailing, its renewal has come about through rediscovery of its original transcendent source of triumphant hope. Hopes are the genes of biblical Christianity. The Bible possesses a multiplicity of eschatologies, no one of which has proven itself the sole model of truth with power to renew the Christian faith. But this we can say for sure: the identity crisis of Christianity today is a reflection of a broader culture crisis in America that manifests itself in a blurred image of an authentic future. Having turned off the lighthouse of eschatology, it can only grope around in the darkness of nationalistic religion and secularized faith.

It is one thing to insist that eschatology is essential to the identity of Christian faith, still another to show its relevance to human existence and the conditions of history. I believe we can and must do theology by correlating the poles of both Christian identity in biblical terms and existential relevance in contemporary terms. So our question is, What does it mean to have an eschatology in human terms? Does eschatology point only to the final revelation of God which we must simply accept by faith or on the basis of authority? Or does it also point to structures of anticipation in human experience which render images of the future meaningful, if not always credible? Is it reasonable to expect the Christian of today,[6] who is also a modern person, to hold to an eschatological faith, if such an orientation is alien to human existence and if there simply are no concepts and categories available to express its meaning and substance?

Eschatological faith was not created *ex nihilo* by New Testament Christianity. It did not fall down from heaven into the hearts of the first believers. The idea of the kingdom of God, for example, was always used by Jesus without further definition. He counted on his contemporaries to be familiar with at least its conventional meanings. But he gave a new shape to the kingdom of God with his life and death, using parables and miracles to pour the wine of new meaning into the skins of old words. What we intend to show, although all too sketchily, is that to have an eschatology is not to go against the grain of human experience, nor does it appear in Christianity without prior preparation in the religious history of mankind.

The roots of eschatological faith lie deep in man's awareness of living within the problematics of time. He may think of the world as permanent and of himself as passing away; or he may think of himself as permanent—at least his soul—and of the world as passing away. Being in the world drives home the inescapable message that we are stretched out in time, pushed by powers that rise up from our past as monsters from the deep and pulled by magnets from the future that lure us into unknown regions. I can sit in my study and know that everything that exists can be found somewhere in space. My mind can wander around in space and imagine places that can be located on the map of the world or the universe. But I can also let my mind wander to the past and recall events that have happened. They do not exist anymore, but they have really happened. They have some kind of reality, not exactly like objects in space, but events of history have their own peculiar way of being real. My mind can also look to the future, to events and situations that have not yet come to pass. They too have their own peculiar way of being real for us. This coming future is so real to us that we spend a lot of our time devising ways and means to control or postpone it, or even to flee from it. Sometimes the impending future seems more real than our past, and more determinative of our actions than the present. "It's a poor sort of memory that only works backwards," says the White Queen in Lewis Carroll's *Through the Looking Glass*.

The prime root of eschatology is this mental fact of reconnoitering not only our whereabouts in space, but also in time, and not only in times past and present, but times coming, the time of the future moving in upon us now. We register the power of this time dimension of the future by our dreams, conscious and unconscious, by our hopes for the future and anxieties about the unknown—the *terra incognita*—by our yearnings and longings for the fulfillment which comes from the future if it is ever to come at all. Only a few desperate souls resign themselves to its never coming, who say "never" to a future much better, and hopefully even infinitely better, than the seemingly all-powerful present.

The existential medium of eschatology in its most primitive form is this power of the imagination to rise above the world as it is—the power of self- and world-transcendence in a modern idiom—to contemplate in images a different and better world. We can know the world as it is; but we can also imagine it quite different, even totally other (*totaliter aliter*).

We have touched on a dualistic factor in the self and its perception of the world. To destroy it is to lose all traces of the meaning of eschatology. A person with an eschatology in the midst of this world is willy nilly a citizen of two worlds. There is this world order, this epoch or aeon, St. Paul says, and then there is the coming world, the new aeon which God is to establish by his power. Without the common human capacity to divide the whole of reality into this extant world of past-present experience and the realm of the coming future, none of Paul's eschatological language makes any sense. Yet Paul wrote as he did because he expected to be understood. He could presuppose that his readers would have a lively sense of that other realm beyond the here and now. Call it what you will—the kingdom of God or eternal life— what matters is that the human condition is marked by this power to imagine the otherness of the future in contrast to the "alreadyness" of the world process. Our traditional dogmatic term for this is the *imago dei*. The image of God in man is this still unextinguished faculty to divine the Divine, to relate ourselves to the absolute future of our lives. In the classical tradition of theology, the image of God has not been totally lost by the fall, but has become perverted beyond human repair.

The image of God in man gives rise to this typical two-dimensional power of the human spirit. It can be expressed in a variety of ways. One way has been classically expressed by Augustine: "Our hearts are restless until they find their rest in Thee." He spoke here as a good Platonist, not distinctively as a Christian. There is an eros deep in the human soul that longs for perfection and fulfillment in an eternal order. A second way is that of existentialist protest: this world is admittedly not what it ought to be, but unfortunately it will never be any different. There is enough transcendence in the human heart to say no to this world, but not enough to construct a positive image of the future. So a person curves in upon his own despair, muttering to himself that things should have been otherwise. In existentialism only the crisis and critique of eschatology remain, none of its attractive and alluring power.

A third line of approach is to look upon this world as a bad dream: the world that we see is only an appearance. To get to what is essentially real we must take an inward journey to the point where everything merges into an undifferentiated unity. This is the way of Asian mysticism, whose spirituality has recently been making inroads into American culture. A fourth attitude is based on a revolutionary model: this world is evil but it can be changed. People don't have to knuckle under to the *status quo* or swallow their protest in quiet despair. They can grasp the levers of change. "The philosophers have only interpreted the world," said Karl Marx, but "the point, however, is to *change* it." These are four typical answers: Platonist, existentialist, Hindu, Marxist. Christianity gives us a distinctively fifth type: in Jesus Christ we have received the word of God's promise that this world will be changed under the impact of his approaching rule. The world may not have utterly changed since the coming of Christ, but now we can live to transform it in light of its promised future in the kingdom of God.

All five views have one thing in common. They refuse to endorse the world as it is. They give off signals of being in touch with another world, either by stark negation of the world as it is or by following a path that leads to the beyond. There is an indispensible element of dualism in all these approaches. The capacity they evidence of transcending the temporal givenness of things is the key to the riddle of the mind that ultimately gives rise to an eschatological consciousness.

It is the function of religion to offer a final solution to the fundamental human problem. This aspect of final solution makes every religion incipiently eschatological in a general sense. Not every orientation to the future drives all the way to the eternal future kingdom which is the core of a complete eschatology. Utopian socialism and scientific futurism are content to point to a foreseeable future in history. The way to this future follows the plan of man. Neither counts on the possibility or necessity of divine intervention. They stress the self-resourcing power and responsibility of man, not the acts of God; they envisage the future of society, not the future of the cosmos; they deal with the penultimate issues of freedom and justice, not the ultimate concern of life and salvation. In pointing to the open horizon of the future, they have nothing to say about death's closing the horizon of life.

THE CHRISTIAN REVISION OF ESCHATOLOGY

Christianity inherited from Israel most of the elements of its own answer to the problems of evil in the world, human sinfulness, and bondage to death. The story of salvation takes place on two levels in the Old Testament. The first is the story of salvation in the history of Israel amidst the nations of the world. The second builds on the microhistory of Israel, the chosen people, using it as a paradigm of the macrodrama of the creation and redemption of the world. The first points to a future in history with the promise of a better life; the second points to a final future of the world in a state of glorious fulfillment. Another feature in Israel's story of salvation is the belief that God will appoint and anoint a special agent—a Messiah—to bring it about. For some Jews this is still an event of an awaited future; many others seem to have abandoned this messianic hope.

Christianity offers an amendment to Jewish eschatology so far-reaching that in effect it entails writing a new constitution for the people of God. This new element is nothing else than the element of radical newness. The promise of the future which Israel has kept alive in her traditions is already manifest in the person of Jesus, the Messiah of God. He is the bringer of a new age, a new covenant, a new community, and a new mission of God for the world. Israel looked to the future for salvation, but Christianity split that future in two, as it split all of time in two between B.C. and A.D. Part of that future arrived in the first coming of Christ; the rest will come at the end of history, when the kingdom of Christ is handed over to the Father. So Christians have their future in the past, because their life is already hidden in Christ through faith, just as they will be given back their past in the future, because in the final resurrection they will enjoy their somatic identities in a state of ultimate and universal fulfillment. They can truly hope to be somebodies forever, not only for a few score years until they are swallowed up by the jaws of death.

All Christian eschatology is united in the affirmation of faith that the final answer to the human predicament has somehow been given in the Christ event. But beyond this point there are numerous schemes of interpretation. We can look at the entire history of Christianity in terms of these various theological models of eschatology. The most important category of distinction is how eschatology relates to history. There are historical and nonhistorical types of eschatology. And each of these can be further distinguished between the Christian and secularized forms.

Historical eschatologies emphasize the time dimension of the eschatological event of salvation. History-oriented eschatology lays hold of salvation in terms of the historical process, at times stressing the *past* as decisive, at other times the *future*.

Past-historical eschatology is radically incarnational, christocentric, and often ecclesiocentric. Eschatology has already been realized in Christ; he is the incarnation of eschatological salvation. The church is the extension of the incarnation. This is the most conservative possible model of eschatology. It fits the orthodox mentality of whatever kind. All important events in God's history with the world have already occurred. The church has only to sit on its past and raise up leaders to function as guardians of the treasury of salvation stored in the documents of Christian antiquity. Nothing new or revolutionary is expected from the future. Orthodoxy pays lip service to the second coming of Christ, but this will only be an unveiling of what lies hidden in the events of the past. The church administers the benefits of this past to all who accept it by faith, in radical dependence on the authorized ministrations of the established church.

Past-historical eschatology has its secularized counterpart in modern liberal Protestantism. Here the incarnation becomes the symbol of a world-historical salvation process that emerges progressively and immanentally through educational, cultural, moral, social, and political enlightenment. Modern process theology is the heir apparent of this liberal conservative-developmental model, holding no great expectations linked to novelties that might apocalyptically reverse the trend of things. For this reason one recent book on process Christology discards the resurrection—which is an apocalyptic event *par excellence*—as not revelant to modern theology. The dimensions of transcendence and futurity in Christian eschatology pose the greatest obstacles to the Christianization of process metaphysics.[7]

Future-historical eschatology affirms the validity of human history for the salvation of mankind. But the center of gravity of salvation history lies in the future. History up to now is prologue, preparatory, prophetic, provisional, or proleptic, and the future has something of its own to bring. In contrast to the incarnational model of eschatology, not the first but the second coming of Christ is the more important for the salvation of the world. This is Christian adventism. It lives in sectarian movements, precisely because orthodoxy has always driven future-oriented believers to the fringes of the church. For the adventists history is not so much the unfolding of what lies hidden in the lap of the past, but a preview of coming attractions, a prolegomenon to the real thing. The future will bring about a totally new situation, a fundamental reversal of the world we know. The main streams of religious life in America were moved by a swift current of future-historical expectation.

An extreme form of future eschatology is represented by apocalypticism. In its popular form the end of the world looms so large that plans for tomorrow become meaningless. The dualism of the two realms is absolute. All the good lies in the future—let all the world be damned! People who hold this view have usually been enlisted from the wretched of the earth. They have nothing to lose but their misery and poverty. It is easy to see how under the impact of secularization this kind of apocalyptic dualism could be continued in Marxism. The violence that apocalypticism prophesied would erupt at the end of the world is brought by Marxism into the dialectics of history as a means to the end.

Nonhistorical eschatologies do not link the coming of the other world to the past or the future but to a timeless present. The eternal now is present in every moment, running along a vertical line from above to below, or from below to above. Eschatological salvation is not a predicate of the historical past or the coming future but is always impinging on the ever-present now of experience. Salvation is available in history for each individual as the eternal word is heard and grasped by faith. But it does not really connect up with the continuities of history, whether as an unfolding of the past or as an anticipation of the future of humanity and the world.

Nonhistorical eschatology can be developed in two different modalities. The first is radically transcendental, the second inwardly existential. In our time the early Karl Barth represented the former, Rudolf

Bultmann the latter.   For the early Barth, eschatological salvation is totally above and beyond history; it is totally other than the world-historical process.   In Barth's memorable phrase, it relates to the world like a tangent touching a circle.   Barth's was a dualism of two worlds standing over against each other, the world of the eternal God above and beyond the world of man here below.[8]   Eschatology which has to do with the future destiny of just this world is lifted into a transcendental realm above it.   The word of the eternal can be heard only within earshot of the point where eternity and time intersect.

Existential-historical eschatology, represented by Bultmann, is equally disinterested in the facts of history so far as the decision for or against the word of salvation is concerned.   What counts is a new existential self-understanding, not the eschatological future of God which relates to the reality of the world as history.   Christian hope is materially empty with respect to the future of the world.   The eschatological images of salvation that embrace the future of man and his world evaporate into the existential now, into the subjectivity of the self and its possibilities for decision.

TOWARD WHOLENESS IN CHRISTIAN MISSION

The typology we have constructed is abstract and is not meant to be an actual description of the current options today.   The aim of the typology is to point out the various ways in which eschatology can be conceptually shaped and their implications for the church's approach to the world.   Our own minimum demand is for a history-oriented eschatology in which the future pole of meaning is kept active in the process of orienting the Christian mission to the world.

Traditionally in dogmatics eschatology was called "the doctrine of the last things."   In our modern revision eschatology deals rather with the ultimate dealings of God with humanity and the world, which the gospel announces to have already begun in Jesus Christ.   Eschatology deals with the ultimate grounds of the possibility of overcoming the negativities of life—"sin, death, and the power of the devil."   Eschatology formulates in symbolic statements the conditions of new life and true being in a liberated world which follow as a consequence of the establishment of God's kingdom, bringing about positive human fulfillment.[9]

The ideas of final judgment, the resurrection of the dead, the end of the world, the advent of Christ, and the kingdom of God are pillar notions of biblical eschatology. As we interpret these eschatological ideas, they are concerned with the conditions for the transition from the old order of things that is breaking down to a new order in which peace, righteousness, and love will reign. They are also concerned with personal, social, and cosmic dimensions of salvation which the gospel promises will be realized in the fullness of God.

The picture of the world as moving from the old order to the new is projected in Scripture as a history of promise oriented to the future. The history of promise in search of fulfillment is conveyed in stories of exodus from bondage, promised land for the wilderness people, homecoming for exiles, liberation for the oppressed, forgiveness for sinners, healing for the sick, peace for the nations, reunion of separated loved ones, resurrection of the dead, and a new heaven and earth for the whole suffering creation. The revelation of God as the maker of promises is the ground of hope that, no matter what, life will be carried through to victory by the power released in the resurrection of Jesus from the dead. Even if the Messiah himself be crucified by the demons of history, God will remember to keep his promises. That is why the resurrection of Jesus Christ is the perpetual source of hope in spite of all the setbacks the people of God experience in history.

The history of promise expands in the biblical traditions, especially in Jewish apocalypticism, to absolutely universal proportions.[10] Monotheistic faith negates every limit to the universality of God's redemptive will.   There is one God—only one ultimate—and he is the Creator of the world, the Lord of history, and the Savior of all humankind.   The vision of universality, however, does not in and of itself produce a missionary faith. What makes biblical faith into a missionary movement is that the universal promise looks to history for its realization. Biblical faith is not universal in an abstract, purely spiritual or mystical sense. It is not reducible to a common religious essence hidden in all the religions, void of all concrete, earthly, historical, and social contents. That is the kind of universalism we find in gnosticism.   Biblical universalism is, by contrast, an historical project. It requires a mission in history to give the universal promise a matching content.

The universal promise of eschatological salvation has not yet been realized in and through history. The meaning of faith in Jesus Christ is to let him be the "Yes and Amen" for all the promises of God (2 Corinthians 1:20). Without him the promise of universal salvation goes begging for credibility and verification. The uniqueness of the Christian gospel and its claim to universal validity rest on the special place that Jesus Christ holds in the structure of history as promise, hope, and absolute fulfillment for all.

The universal promise that is signed and sealed by the life, death, and resurrection of Jesus sets in motion an historical mission to announce and celebrate the universal future that has been opened up for all people, nations, cultures, and religions. None are too bad to be saved or too good to be damned. None are left out of the covenant which God has made and promises to keep on account of Christ.

The deepest root of the Christian mission is thus embedded in the Christian understanding of revelation, salvation, and history, and is not merely an afterthought which dawned on a few Christians who happened to have a vision and heard the Macedonian call. As long as Christian faith is oriented by the history of promise and the eschatological significance of Christ, there will be a Christian mission in world history. Without its roots in the universal promise, missionary faith becomes indistinguishable from religious propaganda.

The universal scope of the history of promise posits the whole world as the horizon of its mission. Person-centered and church-centered approaches are founded on a fundamental dualism, sundering what God has joined together. Consider these familiar dichotomies: religious and secular, church and world, nature and supernature, body and soul, temporal and spiritual, this-worldly and other-worldly, etc. It is disastrous to confine the gospel to one side, isolating the mission and giving priority to individual souls and religious institutions. The mission of faith in the one universal promise is ordained to overcome such dualisms and their destructive effects in world history, precisely because the principle of universality is not a metaphysical idea or mystical feeling. It is something coming into being in an incarnational way and at the somatic level. Mission moves horizontally in world history, and eschews the religious temptation of premature departure from the world through spiritual asceticism or mystical ecstasy.

Person-centered and church-centered approaches to mission, while more or less hung up on a fundamental dualism, turning the gospel in upon the private and religious sector, have always by some happy inconsistency given prime time to the so-called secular aspects, such as schools and hospitals. But they have done this with a kind of bad conscience, believing that their real mission is to save souls and to spread the church. Conceding both the fact and the inevitability of their involvement with the secular world, both Protestants and Catholics have recently tried to revise their missiology, adding the world to their concept of mission. But the world is not something that can be *added* on. The world stands within the horizon of mission from the beginning, or it simply comes too late to prevent evangelistic backlash or ecclesiastical retrenchment. The additive approach appears to be a common-sense middle way between the extremes of pure evangelization and mere humanization, but until the underlying dualism is overcome at the very roots of mission in the universal promise of God, we will still have a bad conscience and inwardly fear the secularization of the church and the loss of what is specifically Christian.

The doctrine of the church needs to be reconceived within the horizon of the eschatological mission of God in world history. The very being of the church is shaped by its missionary calling to go into the uttermost parts of the world. The missionary structure of the church derives from its apostolic origin. The word *apostolic* comes from the Greek *apostello*, meaning "to send forth." The church is sent by the Spirit; the Spirit is sent by the Son, and the Son is sent by the Father. Because church and mission belong together from the beginning, a church without mission or a mission without the church are both contradictions. Such things do exist, but only as pseudostructures. The church becomes a witness against itself when it refuses to criticize its own structures and functions in light of the changing missionary situations in the world.

A church with an identity crisis can do no missionary good. But its true identity is precisely a missionary one. The church's identity does not lie in itself. It can only find itself by losing itself and define itself while being *en route*. It is always in an eccentric position. Nor can the church live merely by reproducing its own traditions. Hence, there must always be something foreign about its mission. It must risk the security of every established identity by being open to new things, practicing creative freedom, experimenting with new possibilities, and entering upon foreign situations. Foreignness is an element of the church's constitution; staying at home is for those in retirement. The church must also have places to care for people too weary to travel—in body, mind, and spirit.

The church's traditional structures, whether congregational, presbyteral, priestly, episcopal, or papal, are not eternal forms of a preexistent institution come down from heaven above. Biblical exegesis, historical research, and the sociology of knowledge have drummed home to us the radical historicity of the church and the relativity of all its structures. What in time became sacral orders were first secular structures in the service of the missionary church. For this reason, the traditional Western churches must be cautious about transplanting their structures in new missionary situations, as though they were timeless and normative for all others. Furthermore, all of the church's structures, even the most primitive, lasting, and useful, stand under the relativizing force of the eschatological future of God's sovereign rule. It is the gospel of the kingdom of God which keeps the pilgrim church humble and deabsolutizes its most hallowed memories and sacred symbols. The debate over the hierarchical form of the church, such as papal primacy, episcopal succession, and priestly ordination, must be conducted within the horizon of this eschatological-historical hermeneutic. Otherwise the debate degenerates hopelessly into self-serving comparison and competition between the churches.

The tension between the institutional church and the missionary church can be overcome by the notion that the church is instituted by God in Christ to be a sacrament of the salvation of the world. The word *sacramentum* is the Latin translation of the Greek *mysterion*. This is the plan of God that is now made manifest through Christ and his friends to the world (Col. 1:26). If we say that the church is the sacrament of universal salvation, this is a confession of hope and not an assertion that can be empirically verified, either with respect to the church or the world. The church is not the salvation of God and it holds no monopoly on the real estate of God's kingdom. But it is a sacrament of eschatological salvation for the whole world. If the church is the sacrament of the world's salvation, she must be open to the reality of the final and universal salvation which she anticipates, celebrates, and prepares for all others. The fullness of this salvation is still to come. Its first fruits, however, can already be enjoyed and shared with the world. People do not have to wait until they are dead before they start living the peace and freedom and righteousness of the kingdom of God.

The individual person and his or her existential experience of salvation is not to be lost in the process of globalizing the Christian mission in world history. In the New Testament the conversion experience—repentance and faith—is not modelled on a psychological form of religious experience. Instead, it is determined by the shape of the kingdom of God. To believe in this God is to take on the shape of messianic life in his crucified representative—election, witness, solidarity, service, and suffering. Trafficking in religious experience—LSD, Transcendental Meditation, the Esalen thing, *I'm OK—You're OK*, the Jesus trip—is not to be equated with faith in the New Testament sense. Faith is no isolated I-Thou relation to God, but includes a double movement of conversion, first to the Lord and then to the world which he loved. There is no way for God and the soul to get along without clasping the hand of the neighbor and doing God's mission together. Faith in God, love to the neighbor, and hope for the world are links in the divine chain of personal conversion.

FOR AND AGAINST THE TWO-KINGDOMS SCHEME

This holistic concept of mission has been hampered by a dualistic model of the kingdom of God which separates the doctrine of salvation from the doctrine of creation. The history of salvation has been isolated from the history of the world. God's message in Christ has been related to the inner life and the afterlife, while other lords and demons have fought for dominion over the body of this life in all its present worldly entailments.

Protestants have inherited a doctrine of two kingdoms which is supposed to do the job of relating eschatological salvation to world history, saving faith in God to loving action in the world, God's redemptive role in Christ to his political purposes in Caesar's realm.   For some Protestants this doctrine of the two kingdoms is one of the untouchables of their tradition.   Our belief is that Lutherans must be willing to take the lead in criticizing this doctrine, perhaps above all others, because the Lutheran record in applying it on the boundary of church and state stinks with the rotting flesh of human beings in jails and concentration camps.   If we respond with the phony apologetic that it's not the fault of the doctrine but only of those Lutherans who misinterpreted it, we are forced to respond that praxis and theory cannot be so easily separated.   We would propose a more dialectical treatment of this doctrine, saying yes and no to certain of its elements.

First, we cannot agree with those who reject the two-kingdoms view *simply* because of its dualism.   A monistic model is inadequate both to the self-transcending dynamics of human existence and to the transcendent revelation of a fulfilling destiny in the life of the world to come. We have seen that any eschatology worth its salt contains a two-dimensional reference, first to human existence in the world as it is and secondly to that eschatological dimension which holds the key to salvation. If the world were saved already, it would look different; if there were no revelation of salvation at all, we could hardly know the difference. But we do know enough to acknowledge the relative difference between what God is doing in the world of business, politics, and culture and what the gospel promises that he has done in Christ for the final salvation of humankind.   Without this bifocal aspect we would bring about a merger of Christianity and civilization such as we have in American civil religion.   By being neither distinctively Christian nor conspicuously civilized it leaves us possibly with the worst of both worlds.   A Christianity that has lost its salt does not much improve the taste of the soup.

Second, we must be decidedly in favor of the simultaneity of Christian existence in the two kingdoms.   Eschatological existence is to be lived under the conditions of world history, offering us no way of escape into another world.   The kingdom of God has arrived in history as the revelation of its end, and not as an alternative to secular life.   The duality does not lead to a split in the person, the soul on an Icarian flight to another realm, and the body dragging along by ball and chain in this one. Such a religion in its extreme form would be indistinguishable from insanity, for it would drive a person not to the splitting of time between the qualities of B.C. and A.D., but to the splitting of the self into the spiritual and the somatic, involving a loss of one's bearings in the world.

Third, the two-kingdoms doctrine is correct in not binding the hands of God to a monomorphous style of acting. God has both law and gospel ways of acting in the world. Without the watchword of dualism, we could slip into a one-dimensional pattern of thinking, making the law into good news and the gospel into bad news. The gospel is the news of good hope that, no matter how pessimistic we may be about the capacity of people and societies for good, God has acted in the exodus of Israel and the resurrection of Jesus to lay a basis for belief in the miracle of transformation of humanity and of all things toward their ultimate fulfillment in the kingdom of God. But the law is also the means of the hidden God to keep people under pressure to meet the minimum demands of justice, to hold nations accountable for their actions, and to stipulate punishment to those who violate the righteous and holy will of God. The judgment of God works its way mysteriously in the course of human events, so that, as Schiller said, the history of the world is the judgment of the world. This is because the Lord of history is immanently at work in, with, and under the events of history as the arbiter of their meaning and final outcome.

Fourth, the two kingdoms are *both* anchored in God's will, so that what goes on in the world is as much his concern as what goes on in the church. There is no such thing as a secular world spinning on its own axis, no such thing as autonomous social, political, and economic structures following their own laws, no such thing as secular authorities who can become a law unto themselves. They are all God's agents in the drama of the world-historical process. God is able to use them, no matter how much they try to screw up the works.

To us this means that God has other servants in the world whom Christians ought to respect. The authorities of this world are not to be feared as little gods, nor condemned as devils. Within appointed limits they can perform the will of God as pressure for good, for freedom, justice, and peace. Bad as it is, this world is God's and he is very much alive within it, even apart from the mediations of Christianity. The world doesn't need Christians to be its businessmen, politicians, and belly dancers. God makes sure we get enough of them, working through the very natural drives we can count on in every human being.

Fifth, the two-kingdoms doctrine is necessary to remind the church of its eschatological identity and mission in world history. If the church hankers to do what every other agency in the world is determined to do, thinking it can do it even better, it runs the risk of neglecting to do the one thing altogether needful—preaching the gospel of Christ—and of doing all the other things in a second best way. We can be sure of one thing: if the church does not preach the gospel of salvation in Christ, no one else will. And of one thing more: if Christians choose not to be the politicians, the businessmen, the labor leaders, the welfare workers, and the military brass hats, others will be around to assume such roles. Christians, of course, are free to seek such offices, but if they do it *at the expense* of their calling to be the elect of God, not only have they betrayed their unique mission but the world is the loser in the end. For the world needs the message of the church, the core of which relativizes the ideas, ideals, idols, and ideologies of the world to keep its horizons open to new ways of embodying God's will for the commonweal. The impact of the ultimate goal on all social achievements keeps them relatively fluid and provisional, and thus never ultimately definitive of the meaning of each individual person. The eschatological horizon of the future lifts up the value of each person before God, making it infinitely disproportional to that person's role in the social whole. A person may therefore seem good for nothing in the eyes of the dominant culture and its decision makers, yet in the light of the Christian message even that person is of absolute worth. His very rights are underwritten by the righteousness of God revealed from heaven.

We have noted crucial arguments in favor of the two-kingdoms perspective. And now the critical points:

First of all, the dualistic element inherent in the temporal and qualitative difference between the finality of the eschatological future kingdom and the provisionality of its present embodiment in the events of history has too often given way to false dichotomies between sacred and secular, spiritual and physical, private and public, religious and political factors in the human world.   The result is that the eschatological kingdom fails to enter this world in all its dimensions, providing neither its critical diagnostic function of prophetic judgment nor its positive therapeutic force for transformation of the areas of life commonly referred to as secular, physical, public, and political.   Eschatological salvation then embraces something less than the totality of life in all its dimensions.   Instead, it is safely enveloped by the private individual and his invisible life of faith, on the one end, and postmarked for a supernatural destination in the life of the world hereafter, on the other.

Second, since so many essential structures of life and history are placed beyond salvation, the church as the elect people with a mission of salvation confines its ministry to the spiritual needs of people and their personal problems.   Important dimensions of the common life are declared out of bounds for the church as the community of the endtime awaiting salvation.   There is then no such thing as social salvation, no social, political, and economic consequences of the gospel in the world.   To be sure, the church allows its individual members to be involved in worldly structures, and as a corporate voice the church may address the public realm.   However, when it does not do so on the basis of the new things (*novissimis*) that have arrived in Jesus Christ, its word can meet the world only on the basis of the old things that presumably reach back to a primordial order of creation and its presumably built-in principles of justice and natural law.   In the public realm the church withholds its word of new things that might touch and incite life in all its dimensions.   Meanwhile it cooperates with the state to keep things the way they are, or if they happen to be in bad need of change, the church may call upon the public authorities to restore them to the level of a prior time.   The past as precedent eclipses the promise of the future.   Nothing fundamentally new is to be expected in the common life of humanity.   Eschatological hopes are made to curve away from the wider horizons of earthly life.   Symbols of salvation which concern the social and political history of mankind are rejected out of hand on account of their utopian affinities and enthusiastic overtones.   If they are permitted any application at all, it is not in the real history of life on earth, but in the life of another world. Thus, eschatology is split wrongly into a dualism of this-worldly and other-worldly spheres.

We affirm the realism of the two-kingdoms doctrine which requires us to take the depth of sin and the power of the demonic seriously in social and political life. This precludes every naive utopianism. When commitment to utopia is challenged by the realities of sin and the demonic, it easily turns into disillusionment and despair, and finally apathy and suicide. But—and this is our third point—the alternative to utopianism does not need to be conservatism, a tell-tale mark of every church impaled on a bifurcation of the two kingdoms. The presence of sin and evil in the world need not render the situation so hopeless that all we can do is build dikes against their chaotic and destructive effects. The ambiguity of life due to sin is just as prevalent in the individual as in the social life. The demons are equally as hard to roust from the religious as the political realm, and the dynamics of judgment and grace are as dialectically efficacious in God's relation to the world as in his relation to the soul. Pessimism concerning the power of the kingdom to transform life in all its dimensions by pointing to sin and evil in the world results in a rationalization of the *status quo* and makes so-called Christian realism a tool of oppression in the hands of those in power.

At stake in deciding for or against a certain theological model of the kingdom of God in history is whether or not we look for the eschatological faith of Christianity to shape the culture of the world and the future of humanity.[11] We believe that the traditional two-kingdoms scheme has fostered the wrong kind of dualism. In that scheme the eschatological kingdom of grace secures the salvation of the individual both here and hereafter, but at the high price of being cut off from the substance of political and social life. The result is two kinds of everything: two kinds of peace, two kinds of justice, two kinds of freedom, two kinds of reconciliation, two kinds of righteousness, and so forth. The love, peace, and righteousness of the eschatological future kingdom are, to be sure, not *of* this world, but they are *in* it, not fully and perfectly, but partly and provisionally, backed by the promise of God to transform the structures of life within the sequences of our history. Eschatological salvation is present in the whole of life, not only in the life of souls. It is still a goal of anticipation in its transcendental character, but even now it can be realized in fragmentary ways.[12]

NOTES

1. Carl E. Braaten, *Eschatology and Ethics* (Minneapolis: Augsburg, 1974).

2. Richard John Neuhaus reports a conversation between Reinhold Niebuhr and Wolfhart Pannenberg as follows: "Driving up to Niebuhr's splendid little apartment overlooking the Hudson River, Pannenberg considered what subject would best be discussed with Niebuhr. The answer seemed obvious: the idea of the Kingdom in Christian theology. It was Niebuhr who had led the attack on the social gospel movement with its idea of extending the Kingdom of God in the social order. Apparently Niebuhr had heard of Pannenberg's work but had not read him. In any case, Pannenberg's question, 'Now, almost fifty years later, do you think the place of the Kingdom in Christian theology should be reconsidered?' met with an unambiguously negative response. 'Social thought that begins with the Kingdom of God, or even emphasizes it very much, inevitably ends up with utopianism. We've been through this business of the Kingdom before.' " "Wolfhart Pannenberg: Profile of a Theologian," *Theology and the Kingdom of God* (Philadelphia: Westminster, 1969), p. 32.

3. See my article, "The Gospel of Justification Sola Fide," *dialog*, (Summer, 1976), Vol. 15, pp. 207–213.

4. Daniel Fleming, *Whither Bound in Missions* (New York, 1925), p. 67.

5. Hans J. Margull, *Hope in Action* (Philadelphia: Fortress, 1962).

6. See Wolfhart Pannenberg, "Can Christianity Do Without an Eschatology?" *The Christian Hope*, Theological Collections, 13 (London: SPCK, 1970), pp. 25–34.

7. John Cobb's most recent book, *Christ in a Pluralistic Age* (Philadelphia: Westminster, 1975), is the most creative attempt to take eschatological themes into a theology structured by the categories of process thought. The spectacle reminds me of putting birds in a cage. The "birds" of biblical eschatology keep on wanting to fly out of the "cage" of Whiteheadian captivity.

8. See Tjarko Stadtland, *Eschatologie und Geschichte in der Theologie des jungen Karl Barth* (Neukirchen/Vluyn: Neukirchener, 1966).

9. I am accepting this definition of eschatology in its basic outline from Wolfhart Pannenberg's treatment in "Eschatology and the Experience of Meaning," *The Idea of God and Human Freedom* (Philadelphia: Westminster, 1973), pp. 197–199.

10. See the discussion on the "universal promise" in the Old Testament by Ludwig Rütti, *Zur Theologie der Mission* (Munich: Chr. Kaiser, 1972), pp. 97–110.

11. The lack of the eschatological dimension of theology is conspicuous in a recent book entitled *The Left Hand of God*, William H. Lazareth ed., with contributions by Gerhard Krodel, Clarence Lee, Oliver Olson, and William Lazareth (Philadelphia: Fortress, 1976). This book purports to be a restatement of a Lutheran social ethic for the American bicentennium. It represents both the pluses and minuses of a typical Lutheran ideology to which we refer in this critique. Lutherans who claim to adhere to the principle of *sola scriptura* should be more open to the findings of biblical theologians concerning the lack of biblical support for the traditional Lutheran two-kingdoms doctrine. I can think of no Old Testament theologians and only a minority voice of German Lutherans who still cling to the two-kingdoms scheme in the interpretation of the biblical materials.

12. Karl Hertz has recently edited a source book of Christian social ethics entitled *Two Kingdoms and One World* (Minneapolis: Augsburg, 1976), in which he provides documents to show that Lutheran theologians in America have produced a variety of revisionist versions of the two-kingdoms doctrine.

3

THE IDENTITY AND MISSION
OF THE CHURCH

CHRISTIAN IDENTITY AND RELEVANCE

Christianity is being confronted by the question of its identity with new sharpness today because of a renewal of other religious options in the world. Bishop Newbigin has said that England is rapidly becoming a Hindu nation. Christianity can no longer assume a religious monopoly in West Europe and the Americas. On the other side, Christianity is being confronted by secular-scientific humanism. World religions and modern humanism—more and more people are leaving Christianity for either of these options, so Christianity is being pressed hard to give a clear account of itself.

The question of Christian identity must be pursued within the horizon of religious and cultural pluralism, where it can no longer be taken for granted that everyone knows what Christianity means, or that Christianity holds the inside track in commanding peoples' interests and loyalties. All the main-line churches have been so busily involved in modernizing their structures and theologies have encouraged such an openness to the world, that Christianity often appears so human, modern, and relevant to the culture in which it stands, that a sense of any difference is lost. Christianity has tried to catch up to the spirit of the times, and has been so successful that it has lost its own distance from the present. It frequently has become nothing but the religious dimension of present-day culture. We have to ask whether this is any longer Christianity, or only a thin Christian covering over the spirit of the age.

Christianity has traditionally carried a message of salvation. Its aim has been to convert the world to Jesus Christ. Nowadays, however, few who call themselves Christian or belong to the church think of Christianity as a dynamic force to change anything in the world. For many it is a halo which the pious wear, a benediction on the world as it is, a compromise with all the powers that be. If our nation is at war, we are there to pray for victory, or at least for the safety of those who fight. Billy Graham is the most popular religious figure in America, and his image is basically supportive of the dominant structures and trends in the nation. He is no radical, despite all his talk about sin and the devil. Nobody really imagines that his preaching threatens to change America in any fundamental way. He is trying to make people into good Christians ready for the second coming.

But if Christianity has lost its world-transforming role, other forces have taken its place. Science and technology are changing the face of the world. Social and political revolution is bent on changing the structures of society to make a better world. If Christianity has lost its power of personal conversion, then other professions—psychology, psychiatry, and various movements of human potential—will fill the vacuum, and do it for profit.

When we ask the question of the identity of the church, we are asking in a roundabout way, what is it that we remember? A person who has suffered amnesia has lost his sense of identity. No one can answer who he is if he fails to remember where he comes from. Loss of memory makes a person disoriented in the present; he has no roots.

The church cannot exist without memory. What is it, above all, that the church has to remember about its very starting point, the origin of its identity? The church has to remember Jesus Christ. "Do this in remembrance of me." The church lives in history by remembering the gospel of Jesus Christ.

This memory is no nostalgia for the good old days, no sentimental desire to go back to the past. The memory is not necessarily pleasant; it can be painful and dangerous. For what we remember can remind us, not how far we have progressed, but how far we have deviated from what is original, decisive, and distinctive in the message of Christ. Such a memory can release judgment on our present and jolt us to change our commitments and priorities. The Christian memory is basic to a critical theory of life, leading to repentance in personal life, church reform, and possibly even revolution in society. The principle of memory has unfortunately fallen into the hands of conservatives, who wish to regiment and regulate the present by the generations of the dead. Jesus, however, said, "Let the dead bury the dead"—a statement which must mean something about freedom in the present, about not being ruled by the generations of the past. This memory principle is not the same thing as a tradition principle which simply links the present to the past as though history can predestinate the possibilities of the future. The Christian memory is rather a subversive principle because it can undermine the powers that be and turn the tables on those who dominate the present.

The Christian memory is the only source of a true and real freedom from the traditions of the past. Without traditions we cannot live, but we can live freely only if there is something greater than a slice of the past to relativize our traditions, even our most hallowed traditions. If what is remembered transcends the tradition, then we are free to have our traditions without being bound to them. Traditionalism tends to mishandle the past by lifting special aspects of it above history, making of them eternal securities. This has often been the fate of dogma, cult, and Bible, of the offices of pastor, bishop, and pope, of moral codes or forms of piety, of particular life-style. The Gothic style in Christianity begins to look like an eternal form when we forget that it is but a tiny piece of human history, and hence possesses no binding claim over our present. It is not the function of memory to restore the past, to re-pristinate outdated theologies, to revive old liturgies, to collect antiques from church history. The function of memory is simply to remember Jesus Christ, "the same yesterday, today, and forever." Because of the continuity of his self-identity, we also remember to read the same book, to celebrate the same meal, and to pray the same prayer. Activating the memory of Christ is the constant amid the variables of the church's involvement in history. If we are slaves to the past, we lose our freedom, but if our memories are enslaved to Christ, we become part of his liberating movement in the world.

The essence of Christianity is not the Bible as such, not the Creeds of the church, not its institutional structures, but Jesus the Christ of God. If we compare Christianity to other religions, we find that they too claim to possess the revelation of God and to bring salvation to their members, but none of them hinges the salvation they have from God to the person of Jesus. If we examine various forms of humanism, scientific or revolutionary, we discover many valuable insights into what is good and just, but none of them find "the way, the truth, and the life" in Jesus Christ.

If Christianity is to be relevant to modern times, then it must be relevant with respect to its own identity principle, not by repeating back to the contemporary world what it finds so good and congenial in it. If the world should come to church and hear nothing but the sound of its own music, the church has failed to let her light shine, to be the salt of the earth, to be the leaven for the rising bread. We can apply this test: if we do in church what others can do just as well, why not let them do it and give them the credit? The one thing which distinguishes the church from the world is the belief that Jesus is the Christ of God and therefore decisive and normative for all matters of faith and life. The church gathers to explore the meaning of Jesus for the way in which we are to understand ourselves as persons, for the way we are to relate to each other as human beings, and also for the way we are to discover what kind of communal and corporate structures are most just for all people and good for the earth. No other group in the world today is holding this conversation about the meaning of Jesus Christ in the world. Only by this conversation can we be assured that the church will not be the world's monkey, imitating its every thought and gesture. This is not to denigrate the world, as though it had nothing to say about that which is true and good and beautiful. Precisely because the world has so much wisdom, the church is tempted to be the world's Sunday morning puppet show, letting the maestros of the world pull the strings behind the backs of Christians. If Jesus Christ is to be the universal Lord of meaning, we are to take all our worldly wisdom and place it on the agenda of our conversation concerning Jesus Christ. All of it can be transformed, converted, baptized, sanctified, and called into the service of Christ's mission in the world. If the church tries to be relevant and forgets to activate its memory concerning Jesus Christ, it has become superfluous. It has become modernized at the cost of its identity.

In recent decades the trademark of much theology and church life has been relevance, modernization, *aggiornamento*. The intention has been to take seriously the existential situation, the historical context, the present-day horizon. Those who would go back on all that are inclined to wrap themselves in a cloak of fundamentalist security. As a community of people in the modern world, Christians do not derive their identity from their environment, nor even from some dimension of depth within them. "You are not your own; you were bought with a price" (1 Cor. 6:19–20).

We cannot answer the modern question, "Who are we?", except in terms of *whose* we are. When we ask about the essence of Christianity, we are tempted to respond in terms of ideas, doctrines, principles, motifs, values, world views, and the like. Such things may be appropriate to other religions, philosophies, and ideologies. But Christianity is linked to the facticity, identity, and meaning of a concrete historical figure, Jesus the Christ of God.

CENTERING THE CHURCH IN CHRIST

The identity of the church is a reflexive identity. It curves back on the person of Jesus Christ, his calling, career, and cross. Since the church will always reflect what it believes about Jesus Christ, it is most important to become clear about the identity and meaning of this person. Who was he? What is his meaning? Many people in the church, even those imbued with the greatest confidence about their personal relation to Jesus, take an unreflective attitude to the question of his identity.

Where do people get their picture of Jesus Christ? From the Bible? That is rarely the case for people tend to encounter the biblical Christ in terms of their own immediate traditions. Without a critical effort, it is very difficult to cut through the layers of piety, ritual, and dogma which time has placed over the biblical picture of Jesus the Christ. The Christ of the Bible tends to be absorbed into the Christ of one's own experience, and whether the two are the same is frequently a question left unasked. But the church must ask the question, lest it trade the *verbum* of the real Christ for some *datum* of its own experience. Then the church becomes its own Lord, bound to its own piety and doctrine, unfit to be the liberating instrument of Christ in the world.

The most important thing for the church to do is to test whether the Christ of its own piety is the real Christ of the Bible.[1] People must become free even to ask such a question. Most people assume, perhaps by an appeal to the Holy Spirit, that the Christ they have experienced is identical with the Christ of apostolic preaching. However, the Christ of piety appears in many different guises. Whose piety is sufficient to paint the image of Christ normative for the church's proclamation and mission? Is it the sweet and handsome Jesus in Sunday church school books? Is it the wounded and bloody figure of Spanish Christianity? Is it liberalism's exemplary teacher of morality? Is it the revolutionary leader of a band of guerrilla fighters intent on driving the Romans from their land? Is it the little baby Jesus in the Christmas story, wrapped in swaddling clothes and lying in a manger?

Piety never comes in pure form; it is always mixed with dogma. So again the question arises whether the dogmatic Christ of the church is identical with the historical Christ of Scripture. Orthodox Christianity always assumed that Jesus could best be interpreted in terms of the trinitarian dogma of Nicaea and the christological dogma of Chalcedon. In this scheme, Jesus is not a human person, but the incarnation of the second person of the Trinity, the Son of God, and therefore the subject of two natures, fully divine and fully human.

In questioning the identity of the Christ of religious experience and the Christ of ecclesiastical dogma, we would not suggest that we could return to a pure historical Jesus free of all later interpretations. We can never encounter naked facts of history minus all the interpretations to which they have given rise. But we can ask whether or not the church can best get its bearings today by reference to the Hellenistic interpretations of Christ at Nicaea and Chalcedon. Liberal Christianity tried to get rid of these interpretations, neglecting the truth they enshrined. We would ask whether it is possible to formulate the same truths in categories not fixed to the language and concepts of Greek philosophy. Is the dogmatic Christ of the Creeds really the only medium through which people in other cultures can encounter the real Christ of the Bible? Does such a Christ make the most sense to people steeped in African and Asian cultures, not to mention our own post-Christian culture in the West?

The church is challenged not only by the living world religions and secular humanism, but also by enthusiastic movements that arise on the fringe and sometimes within its main-line denominations. "Jesus people" and "charismatics" in the church claim to possess the Spirit in a special way which grants them boundless confidence in determining the identity and mission of the church. Over against them stand the ecclesiastical bureaucrats who tend to manage the church in a pragmatic way, thinking of it on a business model as something to make grow and therefore to keep as free of conflict as possible. These bureaucrats are thus basically tolerant of anything that goes on in the church. Thus, too, it is difficult to get the church to make hard decisions that might turn some people off—as in respect to abortion, the gay movement, Vietnam, capitalism, divorce, even the divorce and remarriage of the clergy. If the model of growth that works in business is taken over by the church, then what Jesus Christ was about in his own ministry is basically irrelevant. Certainly he is a poor example to follow, if growth is god of success, because he was a failure in most everything he tried. He died a broken and disheartened individual, not even sure of his own cause: "My God, my God, why hast thou forsaken me?" Did God forsake him? We shudder even to think the blasphemy that escaped from Jesus' lips in that hour of agony.

The proof that we are on the right track in seeking the identity of the church in the person of Jesus can be shown by the way in which every new interpretation of Christianity creates a picture of Jesus in its own image. Even the most progressive theologian who rides the latest wave of culture tries to fill his sails with winds that blow from the shores of historical research into the Gospel reports about Jesus. He also appeals to the historical Jesus, not only to reason, in mitigating his difference from orthodox Christianity. His instinct is basically sound. For what else—barring some latter-day revelation—could convince the church of where to stand than a foothold in the evidence, such as it is, concerning the meaning of Jesus Christ? Should the church throw open its doors to the secular trends of the day? Should it adopt a secular interpretation of the faith? Or should it, on the contrary, deepen its religious sensibilities, and thus make contact with the now fashionable trends of Eastern mysticism? Should it shatter the structures of society, opting for revolution when necessary? Or should it turn inward on the self in search of personal meaning, through T.A. or T.M. or any other bag of tricks that promises health and salvation to the inner man? Should the church flip from social action only to flop into mystical experience? If *Time* magazine covers the story, does that not mean the church should be in hot pursuit of whatever it is that moves people? The caricature is both ludicrous and nauseating. But what else than a solid grasp of what Jesus was about in the world can free the church to be itself, and not a flea market in which every religious huckster can hawk his wares?

The church's identity lies in the right answer to the question, "Who was Jesus Christ?" The Christ defines Jesus, and Jesus defines the meaning of Christ. Ebionitism was an ancient type of interest in Jesus, declared a heresy because it appreciated Jesus as a mere man, as one of the greatest religious personalities of all times. Ebionitism is alive today too whenever Jesus is placed on a line with Buddha, Lao Tse, Mohammed, Karl Marx, or Mao Tse Tung. This is a knowledge of Jesus *kata sarka*, according to the flesh, as Paul said. To know Jesus *kata pneuma*, according to the spirit, is to acknowledge him as the Christ of God.

Docetism lies on the other end of the spectrum. Honor is given to the title of Christ, but each age pours its own religious meanings into it. Christ becomes a symbol representing the presence of God in human life. So there are Christ figures in all the religions, in contemporary plays and novels, and even in modern political life as in the case of Che Guevara. But this does not allow Jesus to define the meaning of the Christ in a decisive way. The title is not uniquely and definitively riveted to the concrete history of Jesus of Nazareth, but fits him like a mask that can just as well be worn by other personalities.

The real Christ of the Bible is Jesus of Nazareth, a man of history, who lived at a specific point in time and at a certain place that can be pin-pointed on the map. Jesus of Nazareth was a Jew, and most of his friends and followers were Jews. Jews never let themselves be taken out of history by myths, such as are found in great abundance in Greece and Egypt and India. The Jews, to be sure, took over some myths from the surrounding religions, particularly those dealing with the creation and end of the world, and certain others which dealt with the incarnation of God and the redemption of mankind. But these myths became drastically reinterpreted in light of the historical experience of Israel and the historical existence of Jesus. The cradle of Christ is primarily history, and myth at best provides some of his swaddling clothes.

The identity of the church does not rest, however, on a lot of historical information about Jesus of Nazareth. Our main sources are the
Gospels, and they notoriously leave out almost everything that a biogra-
pher might want to know about the first thirty years of Jesus' life. We
know as little about the external course of his life as we do about the
internal development of his personality. As Bultmann said, "We can
now know almost nothing concerning the life and personality of Jesus,
since the early Christian sources show no interest in either, are moreover
fragmentary and often legendary; and other sources about Jesus do not
exist."[2] Nothing has changed in the field of historical scholarship to
make us revise Bultmann's seemingly pessimistic verdict. But the Gospels give us all we need to ground the church's identity in the person of
Jesus. They do not give us adequate materials for a biography, but
good examples of the kind of preaching which founded the church,
based on the memories of eye- and ear-witnesses to Jesus. All of these
witnesses portray the ministry of the man in the light of his resurrection.
Without the light of Easter morning the words and deeds of Jesus of
Nazareth would probably have remained eclipsed forever by the black-
out on Friday noon. Only by taking seriously the horizon of faith in the
risen Lord can we understand the meaning of the witnesses to Jesus, the
Messiah, Son of Man, and Son of God. This does not mean that the
history of Jesus in the Gospels is a fabrication of the early church's faith
or that there are only interpretations and no facts. There are no *naked
facts*. The interpretations of faith rest upon real events in the life of
Jesus. The results of the new quest of the historical Jesus make us
relatively sure that there is a life-like analogy between the Jesus of
history and the Christ of faith.[3] The picture of Jesus as the Christ
presented by the believing community was shaped by the impact of the
historical Jesus himself on the memory and imagination of people in his
most intimate circle.

Many people in the church are shaken by the negative implications of
these conclusions. The reports about Jesus in the Gospels cannot be
accepted as historical facts in any modern critical sense. The early
church placed its post-Easter convictions about Jesus into the story of
his life. But faith does not need a stenographic or cinematographic
reproduction of the historical Jesus. All that is essential for the identity

of the church is the assurance that the early church's preaching of Christ is grounded in the real Jesus of history and that its interpretations of his meaning are justified responses to his total impact.[4]   Otherwise the church gets mired down in the suspicion that it lives from a story of its own making or that its picture of Christ is an imaginative retrojection into a make-believe Jesus of history.   Believers want to know that they are the people of Jesus and that his picture in the Gospels was not made in the image of the church.   The history of Jesus himself—his message, life-style and struggle to the end—is filtered to us through the memories and impressions of the early church.   The church's Lord is not an astral deity but the earthly Jesus whose name is passed on through a chain of witnesses that has never been broken.

We have begun to answer the question of Christian identity by looking to the history of Jesus that was cradled in the kerygma of the early church.   We cannot know who we are unless we know where we come from and who gave us our family name, "Christian."   But what does it mean to be a Christian congregation?   That all depends upon what we think of Jesus Christ.   What did he intend?   What did he live and die for?   Was he out to start a revolution?   Or to quell one?   Was he a great champion of law and order and a friend of the establishment?   Or did he throw his weight against those who held power and act like a subversive?   Did he die a heretic or a criminal?   Did he call on people to leave this world for another one, or to share in the mission of God to change this one?   A congregation will place itself in its own religious and cultural setting in a way somewhat analogous to how it sees the role of Jesus in his own time and place.

In the traditions and theologies of some churches Jesus is a man of the establishment.   To invoke the name of Jesus is not to call on a power to scatter the proud, to cast down the mighty, to send the rich empty away (Luke 1:52–53).   Rather, authorities have forged his signature to authorize systems of domination and coercion, even using tools of torture to keep the kind of people Jesus loved in their place. The conservative tradition has made Jesus into a high priest of the establishment, conspiring with the Herods of this world to try those who challenge the system and nail them to the cross.   But Jesus was not a priest, chanting the liturgies of the church and upholding its canon law.

Jesus was not a theologian, neither scribe nor Pharisee, citing sacred precedents of the past to justify the orthodoxy of the present. Jesus was not a church administrator, like the Sadducees, whose meat is to dabble in church politics and to compromise the integrity of the church whenever there are sufficient political or cultural reasons to do so. Jesus was a layman, an itinerant preacher and a popular story teller who depended on friends for meals and lodging. To get where he did, he never earned any credentials or credits and never acquired any union cards, academic degrees, or professional licenses. Today many people would probably call him a bum, a misfit, and, according to our work ethic, a good-for-nothing.

In the traditions and theologies of other churches Jesus is a revolutionary. His message called for fundamental change in the way people are, the values they hold, the goals they seek, how they relate to each other, and in how they run the structures that affect their lives. There is a long line of protesting minorities who have seen Jesus as some kind of revolutionary—early Christian apocalyptics, medieval sectarians, left-wing enthusiasts, as well as today's revolutionary youth and Christian Marxists. Whether this is the right historical image of Jesus is a serious question; the point here is that a Christian community will give an account of its identity in terms of its reading of Jesus' own role in the scheme of things.

Can we as a Christian community derive a revolutionary self-understanding from the model of Jesus? Does *imitatio Christi* mean to be conformed to a revolutionary style of life? Is Christianity a revolutionary movement, or does it provide the world with chaplains to bless every one of its so-called just wars? Our interpretation is this: Jesus was his own kind of revolutionary. The revolution he started does not fit the going models; it is *sui generis*. He mingled with Zealots, used some of their language, and even picked a few recruits from their ranks, but he was not one of them. He shared the popular eschatological hope for the coming of God's kingdom, but he did not translate it into a politics of liberation for the people of Israel from Roman domination. He felt himself to be in solidarity with the wretched of the earth, all the poor and oppressed, but he offered no program of social reform or strategy to redress their grievances. He advanced no hypothesis about this being the best of all possible worlds; he did not explain evil or justify the world as it is. He called for radical change and trusted that God in his own hour would make things right. But he never developed a philosophical theory about causality, explaining how we get from the world as it is to its marvelous future in the kingdom of God. He rejected violence, guerrilla tactics, and military force. He forbade class hatred, vindictiveness, and reprisals. His own severest temptation by the devil was to turn his revolution into a political crusade. He could have become a political messiah, the king of the Jews, and both kick the Romans out and escape the cross to boot. Then he would have forfeited his lasting position as mediator of the kingdom of God in world history. He would have been forgotten about like other revolutionaries in Jewish history.

But Jesus did inaugurate a world revolution which Christians in whatever way they organize themselves are to keep alive. It does not have directly to do with the structures of the church, its cultic practices, system of doctrines, views about morality, degree of piety, and the like. A Christian or a congregation is free to follow its best lights in all these areas, which we might call *adiaphora*. A church body may choose from among congregational, presbyteral, episcopal, or papal structures in ordering its life. A pastor or congregation may be high church, low church, or broad church—and in Japan they would add "no church"— but with none having a claim to superiority. A church confession and its theological tradition may be conservative, liberal, moderate, or radical and still be as Christian as another. People may argue the pros and the cons about the new morality and situation ethics, or they may prefer an old-fashioned code of personal behavior, and we will find revolutionary Christians on all sides of the argument.

So what is so revolutionary about the thing Jesus started? People have jumped on the bandwagon of every revolution that has come down the pike of world history, but they have never been so revolutionary as when they joined the revolution of Jesus. What can be more revolutionary than to love one's enemies? On a personal level Jesus said it means being born again. In terms of national policy it spells the end of war. What can be more revolutionary than forgiving those who do you evil instead of striking back? What can be more revolutionary than to choose suffering for oneself rather than scrounging around for enough power to destroy others?   What can be more revolutionary than to bless those who curse you and do good to those who hate you?   How much easier to do what comes naturally, to go with the adrenalin, joining those who hate and curse and strike and kill all who dare oppose the will of the party and its good causes.   The secret of this new and unheard of revolutionary power Jesus called "the kingdom of God."   The rule of this kingdom in his own life is the deepest ground of the church's identity.   The presence of the kingdom in his own life and ministry is the sufficient reason for the great titles by which he is acknowledged and remembered by the church—Christ, Messiah, Son of man, Son of God, Savior, Lord.

NORMING THE MISSION BY THE GOSPEL

The mission of the church is to proclaim the coming of God's kingdom in the name of Jesus Christ.   God's kingdom, not the church, was central in the message of Jesus.   The church must retain this same priority, with one important difference.   Whereas Jesus looked to the very near future for the breaking forth of God's kingdom, inaugurating an era of righteousness, peace and joy, the church looks back to Jesus, especially to his death and resurrection, as the normative model of the eschatological future of history.   Whereas Jesus preached the kingdom of God, the church preaches Jesus Christ, because already in and through him the ultimate future of all reality has begun to happen.

The absolute future has occurred in history before the end of time, so every historical present is decisively qualified by that event.   Christians are to take the present seriously as the eschatological moment, as though acting in the light of eternity.   This means they are not to live half-heartedly in the present—neither as ascetics nor as cynics—as though all the fullness of life lies in the future.   The eschatological future of God's kingdom did not touch down once upon a time in Jesus, only to leave history with blank pages until its final arrival in power and glory. What is going on between Jesus and the end is the mission of the church to the whole world.

The church does not have only an interpretation of the world; it is involved in the mission of God to change it.   It does not have only a doctrine about the end of time; its vocation is to relativize everything that refuses to acknowledge its own historical relativity. The vessels of the present are not capable of holding the fullness of the future. The prayer for the coming of God's kingdom continues in history. What was begun in Jesus becomes existential for us in the shape of faith, hope, and love. For this reason the church is called to serve the mission of God, running to the world with the message of Jesus about the future of God's approaching kingdom.

It is impossible to enter the kingdom of God without radical change. A person must make an about-face; there must be repentance and faith —a new birth. For what purpose? Shall we say for the sake of God or for the sake of humanity? The gospel of Jesus Christ announces that God has turned the energies of his rule toward the *well-being of humanity*, which the Bible calls salvation. "God will have all men to be saved, and to come unto the knowledge of the truth" (1 Tim. 2:4). The power of God and his kingdom has become *human* reality in the person of Jesus. Therefore, we know that it is the will of God, if not his very nature, to seek the highest possible expression of himself in terms of human existence. We do not have to worry about a hidden will of God outside the realm of the *human*, as though in being really prohuman, we could find ourselves opposed to God.

In spite of the incarnation people find it difficult to think of God and man at the same time. The idea of essential "Godmanhood" does not come naturally. We are more inclined to split the unity of Godmanhood into two separate natures—either God *or* man—rather than to see both together in a single undivided human person. This is not an academic question of keeping one's Chalcedonian categories straight. It bears on the very orientation of the church's mission.

A person enters the ordained ministry of the church, but to what end? To serve God no doubt. But how can a person serve God? God has no needs. But still a person would like to serve him, and not merely be on hand to help one's fellowmen. So perhaps he or she is attracted to the ministry of the church, desiring to play a role in leading the people in the service of God. But how can a person serve God—actually, concretely, and empirically? In this question one encounters the great temptations of all religion.

The first temptation is to translate the service of God into sacred law: God is served by serving his law; we do it zealously by obeying the letter of the law. The idea of God is placed at the head of a vast realm of holy traditions and institutions, ancient laws and commandments, canonical decrees and dogmas which servants of God are to defend and uphold. The mission of the church is to come to the side of law and order, to lend its word and reputation to the offices and institutions that keep things stable and people quiet. God is an archconservative. It is a fact that many sincere Christians cannot see how God could be on the side of the radical left or even sympathetic to the interests of socialists and communists. Our point is not to suggest that the church should opt for one or the other side of the political spectrum. It should be trapped neither by the idolatry of law and order, nor by the spirit of anarchy that seeks their destruction. The church has a norm: the Sabbath was made for man, not man for the Sabbath. Laws are meant for the good of people, not as chains to bind their freedom. Man *is* the measure of all things, especially of all the laws that have been handed down in the name of God—with this proviso: that Jesus Christ is our definition of what it means to be truly human, *vere homo*!

The second temptation for those who are part of God's mission is to translate it into ritual ceremony. The world is split into religious and secular realms, and the church is driven by inner and outer forces to stick to a religious agenda. Whatever goes on in church is its prime business, such as Sunday morning worship and other ceremonies— baptism, confirmation, marriage, and burial. The vast secular world of government, business, education, and medicine is alien territory into which the church strays at her peril. But the church's unified mission is to break down the wall of partition between the religious and the secular. Love of the neighbor is the criterion of a sincere love of God. The story of the Good Samaritan shows how the man who helps his neighbor pleases God, whereas the priest who passed by on the other side was no doubt on his way to a church meeting.

The history of Christianity is filled with accounts of the church betraying its Lord and contradicting its mission of service to the kingdom of God. How can the church today discover its true world mission in a way faithful to its original historic identity? We can speak of this search for its real and full mission as *the norming of the church*. Our argument thus far has been to show that Jesus preached the kingdom of God, which is not identical with the church. He counted on its coming in his immediate future, and therefore set up no constitution for an organized church. It is indeed doubtful that his vision of the future included a plan for the church as a separate community of people to be cut off from Israel. As Jesus said, "I was sent only to the lost sheep of the house of Israel" (Matt. 15:24).

Although Jesus was not the founder of a new religion, he is the foundation of the Christian faith—"the church's one foundation." The historical riddle of how the church came into being in lieu of the kingdom of God which Jesus awaited is one of the great mysteries of which we shall perhaps forever remain ignorant. Why did God disappoint Jesus and give him a cross instead? How could the death of this man Jesus, however noble, good, and true, explode into a world-historical movement, making Christianity today the one truly universal religion of mankind? This has to do with the resurrection and faith. On account of the resurrection, Jesus is not merely the past-historical foundation of Christianity, but also the present risen, living Lord of the church and the world. Jesus is not the founder of the church merely as its model and example, like the founding heroes of other religions. He lives now as the crucified and risen Jesus in the world.

What does this make of the church? The church is the community of persons who live by the knowledge of faith in the crucified and risen Christ. There was no church before Good Friday and Easter. The power of the Spirit was released at Pentecost to integrate the recollections of the early Christians about Jesus into its picture of the risen Christ—the permanent foundation of the church (John 14:26). The mission of the church must forever be normed by its relationship to the total picture of Jesus Christ.

If the church is to follow the christological norm of mission, she has to struggle for the realization of the kingdom of God on the model of its definitive arrival in Jesus Christ. Is the present-day church norming its mission on such a model, or does it make up a program of convenience to suit itself? This is a question for the church as a whole as well as for each congregation of believers. For what we mean by church includes both a universal and a particular pole of reference. The church as a reality in world history is not only a name (nominalism) for the sum of its individual parts, namely, local congregations. And the local congregation is not merely a fragment of the whole church of Christ: where Christ is present, there is the church. The whole church is present in each of its local instances on account of the real presence of Christ, who as the head cannot be separated from all the members sharing the life of his body.

In the present ecumenical dialogue Protestants have been rediscovering the fullness of the church with the stimulus of their Catholic brethren. Many Protestants have had a "little-flock" mentality. Their concept of the church is modeled on the saying of Jesus, "Where two or three are gathered together in my name, there am I in the midst of them" (Matt. 18:20). This has given Protestants a sense of the particularity of the church. The church, properly speaking, is not a massive network of organizations and officeholders spread around the world, but the concrete occurrence of the word in this particular community. It is the communion with Christ in, with, and under *this* loaf of bread and *this* cup of wine, the healing going on among those—the Joes and Janes and Toms and Alices—who gather regularly on *this* corner of Main Street.

However, this Protestant emphasis has proven deficient for a full understanding of the church. The Protestant style has tended to be schismatic, sectarian, individualistic, subjectivistic, and parochial. Each congregation has been left pretty much on its own, at the mercy of little popes who indulge their lust for power. The separate congregation also, as a little ship on the high seas, is likely to be tossed about by the winds and waves of its surrounding culture. Without the ballast of the whole church to stabilize its course, the little ship may too easily capsize on the waves of racism, fascism, militarism, materialism, secularism, or whatever prevailing *Zeitgeist*. The substance of the universal church can provide the local congregation with resources for a richer experience of the people of God in history, uniting it with saints of other times and places who despite great varieties of language, culture, and ethnic identity, are held together by a common faith in the same Name, the same Lord and Savior, the same word of God in Scripture and tradition, the same washing of regeneration, the same eucharistic meal, and the same brotherly love. The church's mission, therefore, can be guided by the principles of both Protestant particularity and Catholic universality.

The mission of the church to the world begins at home. The good news it has to broadcast to the nations is an inner-churchly imperative. Consider the great ideals of the French Revolution: liberty, equality, and fraternity. These social goals were first mediated to Western culture by the preaching going on in the church—not that the church ever practiced what it preached. Very often the church has been behind society in realizing the meaning of its own proclamations. Yet, even in darkest times the church has transmitted a tradition of images and ideals that place it under judgment and move people to dream and struggle for a new and better world. This is what happened at the time of the Enlightenment. The vision of new life in Christ—embracing freedom, equality, and brotherhood—was translated from abstract imagery to concrete reality, from the cloistered realm of religion to secular society. As they become secularized these general social goals run the risk of becoming empty slogans, as is perfectly evident in expressions like "the free world," "free enterprise," "religious freedom," and the like. They need to be renewed and redeemed by tracing them to their roots in the gospel of Jesus Christ.

Freedom is one of the core concepts of the gospel. Christ has set us free to be the children of freedom. The church can hardly proclaim liberty to the captives (Isa. 61:1 and Luke 4:18) and then pursue an authoritarian style in running her own affairs.

The gospel also means equality. In spite of moral gradations among people, all are sinners and are accepted by grace alone. No one possesses a righteousness of his own that meets the standard of divine justice. The gospel is thus bad news to tyrants who deny the fundamental equality of all people before God, bad news to those who would carry the distinctions of race or class or caste into the life of the church. In the new community of Christ let none be ranked according to their works or merits; let the church remember its norm. Those who are first will be last, and the last will be first. Let the leader stoop down to serve the people and not sit on a high and mighty throne.

The world should be able to look upon the church and say, "Look how they love one another." Christians are to deal with each other like brothers and sisters, in trust and openness, whether rich or poor, black or white, slave or free, cultured or untutored, urban or rural, liberal or conservative, religious or secular. All are free and equal members of the one family of God.

The church cannot give to the world that in which she has no share. The gospel of Christ brings with it a promise for the unity of mankind. The church is a community of persons who already share the eschatological unity of mankind represented by Christ. In real life, however, Christians and churches bear the marks of fragmentation and alienation from each other. In the recent past we have heard a lot of ecumenical talk about the scandal of divisions. Leaders of the ecumenical movement have spoken glowingly about the coming great church. Today, however, many have lost their zeal for ecumenism, giving way instead to a resurgence of denominationalism and ethnocentricity. But the meaning of the ecumenical movement is not merely that of getting likeminded Christians together in one big happy family. The ecumenical movement is more profoundly linked to the world-historical mission of the church to represent in a proleptic way the unity of all mankind in the kingdom of God. The reunion of Catholic, Orthodox, and Protestant churches in some sort of ecclesial association that witnesses to the universal unity of believers in Christ is an imperative that stems from the eschatological vision of the church and its mission in the world.

THE IDENTITY CRISIS IN MISSIONS TODAY

The Christian world mission is suffering from its most acute identity crisis since the beginning of the modern missionary era. The whole missionary idea—long believed to be based on the command of Jesus to go into the whole world and preach a gospel of salvation with unconditional validity and universal scope—is being called into question. The image of the Western missionary is at an all-time low. In the movies, where many images are decisively formed, he is pictured as a narrow-minded bigot with a Bible, wearing a white suit and a cork hat, trying to convert "noble savages" who live an idyllic life unspoiled by the white man's ideas.

But beyond the popular level the Western and American style of the

Christian mission is being radically criticized. The sharpest voices are coming from the Third World, from the very fields in which the Western theology of mission has been practiced with the greatest results. We could almost formulate a law to the effect that where the Christian mission has succeeded the most, there the greatest awareness of its failure prevails. The end of the missionary era! What is that but a just fate shared by all forms of Western colonialism and imperialism? Nevertheless, the irony of the gospel may also be hidden in the same set of historical facts, an irony that signals the victory of the gospel in the shape of the cross. The crucifixion of the Christian mission in our time may be the essential medium for the hope of its resurrection in new forms of spiritual power and universal validity.

But the crucifixion comes first, from Asia, Africa, and South America! In *The Christian Century*, Fr. Paul Verghese of the Syrian Orthodox Church in India writes: "The mission of the Church is the greatest enemy of the Gospel."[5] Another Asian voice, Emerito P. Nacpil, president of Union Theological Seminary in the Philippines, charges that the missionary today is "a symbol of the universality of Western imperialism among the rising generations of the Third World. Therefore I believe that the present structure of modern missions is dead. . . . The most *missionary* service a missionary under the present system can do today in Asia is to go home."[6]

Africa, too, has raised its voice. The Assembly of the All Africa Conference of Churches, held at Lusaka, Zambia, May 12–23, 1974, called for a moratorium—a complete halt—on the receiving of money and personnel from overseas churches. The purpose is to erase every trace of domination over the weak churches in poor nations by the strong churches in rich nations. The churches in Africa want to get rid of all religious remnants of colonialism, to make African Christianity free of the religious dimension of cultural imperialism and authentically African. Interpreting the message of this moratorium Canon Burgess Carr, an African Anglican churchman, writes, "It is clear that we will never be self-reliant as long as we maintain the structures that we inherited from expatriate missionaries."[7]

Voices from Latin America sound a similar note. The World Council of Churches sponsored a symposium of anthropologists on the subject of "Inter-Ethnic Conflict in South America," in Barbados, January 20–25, 1971. Out of it came the "Declaration of Barbados," which concluded from its findings that "the suspension of all missionary activity is the most appropriate policy on behalf of both Indian society as well as the moral integrity of the churches involved."[8] This declaration claims that the process of evangelization gives a religious pretext for continuing the colonial situation and functions as a mechanism of exploitation and alienation of Indian society.

One of the earliest and boldest demands for a moratorium on mission American style came from Ivan Illich. As early as 1967 he wrote "The Seamy Side of Charity" in *America*, detailing the negative results of foreign ideas, foreign dollars, and foreign missionaries in South America, thus blunting the call of the Catholic hierarchy for twenty thousand new missioners south of the border. Ivan Illich said that all this foreign generosity was making the church in Latin America a satellite of North Atlantic Christianity—"a colonial plant that blooms because of foreign cultivation."[9] Illich uses strong language, speaking of missionaries as "pawns in a world ideological struggle," "projecting the image of U.S. outposts," "undercover agents, albeit unconscious, for U.S. social and political consensus."[10]

More currently the liberation theologians of South America have released an avalanche of criticism, like Illich linking the missionary enterprise to Western European and North American structures of economic, political, cultural, and technological domination. Not only neo-Marxists like Gustavo Gutierrez[11] but a conservative evangelical like Orlando E. Costas hold it as now self-evident that the "missionary enterprise has been used as a justification and cover for the domination of people. The interrelation between mission, technology, and imperialism is well known. The expansionistic ambitions of militarily and economically powerful countries have always been accompanied by a missionary interest."[12] An Asian theologian, Kosuke Koyama, describes this tie between mission and imperialism in an appropriately worded title, " 'Gun' and 'Ointment' in Asia," showing how each reinforced the claims of the other.[13] José Miguez-Bonino, Argentine Methodist theologian, writes that "the real problem is that the alliance of missions and

Western capitalistic expansion has distorted the gospel beyond recognition."[14] If the mission of the church, Miguez-Bonino goes on to say, is to join the struggle for the liberation of people in the Third World, it will have to pitch itself "against the policies and interests of this country (the USA), at least against the policies and interests that dominate this country. It is not merely this or that exceptional economic concern or military program that we have to resist; it is an entire system that concerns local tyranny in our own Third World in foreign interests, economic exploitation, military repression, and cultural brainwashing, to perpetrate oppression. Many of you and many of us are knowingly or unknowingly part of that system."[15]

We have given only a few samples of the heavy attacks aimed at the traditional Christian mission. American Christianity has invested too much of its soul in the modern missionary movement to accept these Third World criticisms at face value. We can expect that efforts will be made to revive some of the old evangelistic zeal for American missions abroad and thus to get back to business as usual. We can expect that all the bad news from the Third World will be read as a mere echo of the classical Marxist-Leninist criticism that Christian missions are a form of imperialism. To many Christians the gospel and their own identity as Americans are so fused that an attack on American imperialism will be met as a plot of the Anti-Christ.

We are entering, in the churches, into a period of painful polarization on the issue of Christian mission. The polarization is taking the shape of antagonism between the evangelical-minded and the ecumenical-minded branches of Christianity. The ecumenical theology of mission has been worked out and expressed in the most recent ecumenical conferences. At Mexico City in 1963 the Commission on World Mission and Ecumenism developed the concept of "mission on all six continents." This broke down the distinction between home missions and foreign missions, between missionary-sending churches and mission fields. All churches are missionary and the mission field is everywhere. At Uppsala in 1968 the *bon mot* became "humanization" as the goal of the Christian mission. The gospel has to do with power structures that affect the quality of human life and not only personal decisions. At

Bangkok in 1973 the conference theme was on salvation, interpreted as liberation from economic injustice, political oppression, social alienation, and personal despair.

It is clear that the developing ecumenical theology of mission would be open to and even reinforce the criticisms of mission emanating from the Third World. As the Third World churches increase their membership and participation in the ecumenical structures, we can expect the spotlight of criticism to become focused more sharply on Western and American ventures in world mission, exposing all of their close historic ties to colonialism, capitalism, and cultural imperialism.

On the other side the evangelicals are extremely critical of the ecumenical trend toward defining mission as the process of humanization or liberation within the horizon of this world and its inner-historical future. The evangelicals would still speak of mission as evangelism leading to personal conversion and eternal salvation. They stress this as the prior, though not the only, concern of the church in mission. The things that the ecumenical people are stressing may be indirectly the concern of evangelism and mission, namely, the ethical by-products of Christianity lived in the world. The evangelicals met in the summer of 1974 in Lausanne, Switzerland, summoned by Billy Graham and other Protestant evangelical leaders to an "International Congress on World Evangelization." The results of it was "The Lausanne Covenant." The church-political intention of this was to juxtapose an evangelical consensus on mission against the mission trends promoted by the ecumenical leaders in Geneva. While this Covenant makes mention of the humanistic, historical, and social aims of ecumenical missiology, they are definitely relegated to secondary status.

This repristination of the conservative evangelical position on mission, whatever its Christian motives, runs the risk of providing ideological support to the traditional Western and American patterns of intervention and involvement in the underdeveloped nations. If economic, political, social, and cultural dimensions of human life are not incorporated integrally and holistically into the essence of evangelism and the substance of salvation, they become the playing field of other powers, other gods and idols, other ideologies and world views. Then the Christian mission has priced its salvation too high for human beings, too far above and beyond the level of history where humans struggle for life. Salvation becomes a purely other-worldly thing, out of sight and out of reach, serving the interests of the established order to keep things stationary or at least under the control of the dominions that rule the present. The polarization between the evangelical and ecumenical statements on mission is not merely an internal squabble among Christians or a harmless game that theologians play. There is always some political fallout from the rockets of religious dissension, and these will have effects of global magnitude.

The present confusion in mission has deep roots in the convictional symbol systems that moved Christians to cross frontiers and work in strange lands. Someone has said that in the past the missions always had problems, but today the mission itself has become a problem.[16] There is no one answer to the question: What is the Christian mission? Our description of the Christian mission within the present world situation tries to embrace both the passion of the evangelicals for the uniqueness of the Christian message and the vision of the ecumenists for the universality of its scope. We hope we can take up the valid motifs in past and present theologies of mission, in order to place them in a more comprehensive framework and thus overcome their one-sided and reductionistic character. The basic task is to renew the missionary dimension of the gospel and our commitment to it within the horizon of a critical global consciousness that takes seriously the criticisms of the Third World.

The dilemma we in the American church face is that theology is challenging us to renew our missionary consciousness at a time when others, especially in the Third World, are calling for the end of the missionary era. The dilemma is this: if we are true to the gospel of God's universal promise in Christ, we will be a missionary church, but under present conditions we are burdened by *impedimenta Americana.* When the early church became established in the Roman Empire under Constantine, it became imperial, triumphalistic, authoritarian, and expansively ecclesiocentric, losing its missionary identity and structure. If we do not succeed in cutting the ties between the Christian mission and American imperialism, we will bring a moratorium of missionary action upon ourselves as we did in China, where the number of missionaries went from ten thousand to zero in a few years.

The task ahead is to descandalize the form of the Christian mission without removing the scandal of the gospel itself. There will always be something foreign about the Christian mission—we are driven by it beyond ourselves. Its message meets us in our native condition as an alien thing, either as a stumbling block or as foolishness, which we can surmount only by radically transcending ourselves. For this reason, a purely horizontal streamlining of the mission as humanization may be a sellout, recalling H. Richard Niebuhr's characterization of the preaching of liberalism: "A God without wrath brought men without sin into a kingdom without judgment through the ministrations of a Christ without a cross."[17]

Removing the wrong scandal will involve Americans in maintaining a low profile within international structures of world mission. The largest portion of money must still come from the rich churches—with no strings attached—but now they must send a minority of personnel. If, however, the main-line churches of the West insist on dominating the missionary enterprise in Third World situations, like the rich young ruler, they will be sent away sad. Only by internationalizing the teams that cross the frontiers of nations and cultures, can the imperialist, colonialist, or capitalist image of the Christian mission be effaced. Such a format makes possible a double witness: to the promised unity of humankind through the power of the gospel, and to the radical pluralism of the one body with its many different members. Western European and especially North American churches—attached as they are to inherently exploitative systems of life—may have to move more passively abroad and more actively at home. How can the American denominations expect to cross the racial, cultural, and economic barriers abroad, when their experience at home proves that their white, affluent, middle, or upper class status creates a gap they have not yet effectively bridged?

Many Americans will welcome the word that they can stay home and do mission in their own backyard. Neoisolationism in politics can easily be transferred to religion. The American church is already in grave danger of falling into the Babylonian captivity of civil religion. In the fifties we thought we were emerging out of that, but now in the seventies it has become fashionable again. To prevent this we must take up what Gustavo Gutierrez calls a "conscienticizing evangelization."[18] This is evangelism based on the revolutionary thrust of the gospel. It involves making the whole people of God aware of the terrible injustices perpetrated by our own social, political, and economic systems both upon the proletariat of the poor in our nation and upon the external proletariat of Third World peoples. It is not enough to accept the moratorium demanded by the more radical voices in the younger churches; that could result in doing nothing. Speaking of the church in mission, Gutierrez says, "Its greatest 'o-mission' would be to turn in upon itself."[19]

Conscienticizing the mission will mean something more than saving souls and planting churches; it will mean something more than emergency relief and charitable works. Mission will assume the role of advocacy, tracking down causes of global injustice and violence. Mission funds should be used in research, not only on how better to train missionaries or to open new fields, but as to how the American system itself, in which we are enmeshed, is involved in a conspiracy with other big powers to control and channel the world's limited resources to our own advantage. As never before the ethical side of evangelism and the political meaning of eschatology must be worked out on a planetary scale. If faith is radical dependence on God, mission is total interdependence among people, overcoming all idolatry in the one case, and all systems of domination, oppression, and exploitation of the many by the few in the other.

If the church is God's agent to proclaim the coming of God's kingdom as the hope of the world, particularly in the cruciform of the gospel of Christ, can we imagine some of the forms its mission might take in our time and place?

A congregation must develop a bifocal approach to mission, keeping in view both its local situation and the global scope. The idea that we are living in a global village cannot be shrugged off as futuristic dreaming. The Vietnam war, the energy crisis, the food shortage, Henry Kissinger's travels, the Olympic games, and the evening news make us conscious that we are citizens of this planetary age. A congregation must ask about the international outcome of its own missionary commitment. For example, if a congregation answers the call to help resettle a Vietnamese refugee who was running away from communism but turns a deaf ear to the Chilean refugees who are forced out by a fascist military junta, then it is letting its missionary policy be dictated by political ideology and not evangelical love. A well-intended act of charity has far-reaching international implications. When Christian agencies working among orphans in Vietnam smuggled many orphans out of Vietnam in the last critical days so they would not grow up among godless communists, their decision was probably a contradictory mixture of good gospel and inhuman politics.

It will no longer do for congregations to play only an indirect role in the worldwide mission of the church. It used to be that a congregation was a place missionaries would occasionally visit, tell a few exotic stories from the mission field, ask for both money and prayers and flee. Today the congregation must find a way of involving itself in the "mission on six continents." The global horizon of mission is not for a few lifetime professionals. Mormons send out two by two, and they all take their turns. Other churches have gone more to short-term project-oriented missionaries, so that more and more lay people are getting firsthand experience at bearing the good news in places far from home.

Another facet of mission for the local congregation is to find ways of receiving the missionary witness of members of the so-called younger churches. The traffic has always gone one way from the West to the East and the North to the South. Now is the time for two-way traffic to begin. Many congregations have so locked Christianity into their own one-dimensional culture, they can hardly imagine what it would be like to be Christian in other cultural situations. Meeting Christians of the younger churches in Third World countries who are socialists, and sometimes even Marxists, is a challenge to our simplistic identification of the values of Western culture with Christianity.

A third dimension of mission is to penetrate the particular socio-cultural ambience of a congregation in a critical way. The alternative to culture-Christianity is not withdrawal and detachment, but responsible and critical involvement. This is to practice the economy of the incarnation—the model of Christ. This cannot be done abstractly in global terms, but in terms of concrete negations of the local conditions that obstruct the rule of God's kingdom and its qualities of freedom, peace, and justice in a particular neighborhood. The power of negative thinking, to use Herbert Marcuse's term, must be kept vital in the prophetic ministry of the church.

A fourth aspect of mission is apologetic. The church must witness to the truth of the gospel in a post-Christian society, where the problem is one of overexposure. The world is filled with ex-Christians who claim to have had it with the church. Some of them still believe in God and love Jesus, but prefer to keep their distance from the church. Winning back these people can be done only through a dialogical form of ministry, in which their own reasons for leaving the church are taken seriously and resolved into a higher synthesis of understanding. Such people cannot be expected to return to a naive intransitive consciousness over against the Christian faith. Faith for them is not so much a matter of holding unconditionally to the eternal verities, but a process of inquiring into the reasons of faith and of critically debunking illusions which commonly lead people astray.

A closely related function of mission is to participate in the common struggle for the promotion of what is human. Jesse Jackson is the head of PUSH—People United to Save Humanity. But he preaches about jobs, housing, schooling, welfare, health, violence, law enforcement, drugs, and everything else that impinges on the quality of life in the city of Chicago. Social progress and economic development cannot be separated from spiritual life as in the two-kingdoms doctrine. If the plight of black people makes it impossible for Jesse Jackson to keep politics out of preaching, is it fundamentally any different in white society? Can preaching be separated from the common effort to make human life more human? There is nothing too secular for Christian concern. All things are to be taken captive to Jesus Christ as Lord— for the common human good.

It is perhaps always necessary to repeat to ourselves that although the proclamation of the gospel is the one and only mission of the church to the world, this is never just a matter of the right verbalization of biblical and Christian ideas. Words and deeds belong together. Therefore, evangelization and humanization belong together, and so do gospel and social concern, faith and political action, religious worship and secular work. We cannot share the view of those who insist on the primacy of evangelization, if by that they mean to separate what Christians say from what they do. For the gospel is not only something to be said, but is itself an action of God in the world, taking the form of both evangelical word and apostolic deed.

NOTES

1. I am reflecting here Martin Kähler's concept of the "whole Christ of the whole Bible" which provided the theological backdrop for his critique of the half-Christs of the numerous modernizing and psychologizing biographies. Kähler's criticism of the "lives of Jesus" antedated Albert Schweitzer's by more than a decade. See Martin Kähler, *The So-Called Historical Jesus and the Historic, Biblical Christ* (Philadelphia: Fortress, 1964).

2. Rudolf Bultmann, *Jesus and the Word* (New York: Charles Scribner's Sons, 1934), p. 8.

3. This idea of "life-like analogy" is intended to convey what Paul Tillich meant by *analogia imaginis*. The background of Tillich's notion can be found in Martin Kähler, whose influence on his christological thought Tillich acknowledged on numerous occasions.

4. The post-Bultmannian "new quest of the historical Jesus" was right in seeking to ground the Christology of the early church in the ministry of Jesus of Nazareth, using every possible means of historical research and imagination. Its success, however, was restricted by the influence of Heidegger on Bultmann's pupils among whom the need for a "new quest" was so keenly felt.

5. Paul Verghese, "A Sacramental Humanism," *The Christian Century,* September 23, 1970, 1118–1119.

6. Emerito P. Nacpil, "Mission but not Missionaries," *International Review of Missions,* July, 1971, pp. 358–360.

7. Burgess Carr, "The Moratorium: The Search for Self-Reliance and Authenticity," *All-Africa Conference of Churches Bulletin,* Vol. VII, No. 3, 42.

8. "The Declaration of Barbados," *The Gospel and Frontier Peoples,* R. Pierce Beaver, ed. (William Carey Library, 1973), pp. 369–375.

9. Ivan Illich, "The Seamy Side of Charity," *The Church, Change and Development* (Chicago: Urban Training Center, 1970), p. 25.

10. *Ibid.*, pp. 30, 31.

11. Gustavo Gutierrez, *A Theology of Liberation* (MaryKnoll: Orbis, 1973).

12. Orlando E. Costas, *The Church and Its Mission: A Shattering Critique from the Third World* (Wheaton: Tyndale, 1974), p. 245.

13. Kosuke Koyama, " 'Gun' and 'Ointment' in Asia," in *The Future of the Christian World Mission,* William J. Danker and Wi Jo Kang eds., (Grand Rapids: Eerdmans, 1971), pp. 43 ff.

14. José Miguez-Bonino, "The Present Crisis in Mission," *Mission Trends No. 1,* Gerald H. Anderson and Thomas F. Stransky eds., (Grand Rapids: Eerdmans, 1974), p. 41.

15. *Ibid.*, p. 44.

16. The statement has been attributed to the German missiologist, Walter Freytag.

17. H. Richard Niebuhr, *The Kingdom of God in America* (New York: Harper and Brothers, 1937), p. 193.

18. Gustavo Gutierrez, *A Theology of Liberation,* p. 116.

19. *Ibid.*, p. 138.

4

THE GOSPEL OF SALVATION
AND THE WORLD RELIGIONS

CHRIST: THE LORD OF HISTORY

The Christian who is also an historian faces the dilemma of having to be loyal to two masters.[1] As a Christian he is heir to the confession of Jesus Christ as the Lord of history; as an historian he handles the data of history with the critical tools of historical science. Committed to these two loyalties, one symbolized by Christ the meaning of history and the other by Clio the muse of history, the believing historian experiences the clash of spirit in his mind and heart.

St. Augustine succeeded in baptizing the Greek muse and placed her in the service of a theological interpretation of world history. Origen, too, in his debate with Celsus, the pagan intellectual, interpreted all of history as the unfolding of divine providence and pedagogy. In the twelfth century Joachim de Flore presented a three-fold periodization of history reflecting the doctrine of the Trinity. It was not until the Renaissance that history began to declare its independence from Christian dogma. During the Enlightenment the discipline of history overthrew its theological master in exchange for a philosophical dictator. Not faith but reason was supposed to generate the light for interpreting the meaning and movements of history. The shift from a theology to a philosophy of history—something which happened almost imperceptibly in Hegel—was the wedge which widened the breach between Christian faith and secularized reason. It was not long, however, before history as an aspiring science would clamor for a total emancipation from philosophy as well. Every kind of transcendentalism in the interpretation of history would be condemned as an escape from the realities of history. Such a positivistic approach to history has been called historicism. In aiming to be a science, nineteenth-century historiography fashioned itself on the model of the natural sciences.

The Christian historian may rejoice that the rationalistic philosophies of history have been ambushed by the scientific approach to history. Philosophies of history were often thinly-veiled secularizations of theology, advancing the interests of neither science nor faith. However, the decline of confidence in the philosophy of history does not signal a return to the idea of a theology of world history. The spirit of positivistic historicism is as remote from the idea of God acting through history as from the philosophical idea of an immanent teleology manifest in the particular events and changing structures of history. The mood of historical science is not congenial to a revival of a Christian interpretation of history.

Against the stream of the secular mind a number of twentieth-century thinkers have nonetheless essayed a theology of history, notably people like Berdyaev, Tillich, R. Niebuhr, Butterfield, Dawson, Löwith, and others. Today we witness a renewal of the attempt in such diverse programs as Wolfhart Pannenberg's theology of universal history and Gustavo Gutierrez's theology of history as the liberation of oppressed peoples. There is obviously no inclination on the part of Christian theologians to abandon history. As Christians they acknowledge that Christianity ceases to be Christian the moment that it takes a flight from history. The Christian revelation is bound up with the stuff of history.

The theologians of history, however, tend not to be card-carrying historians. They surely deal with the facts of history, but refuse to confine themselves to the system of categories and axioms of history as a secular science. One secular historian has said that their solution to the problem of history "is in keeping with the revival of antirational modes of thought in general. . . . Ultimately, their solution expresses the same mood of defeat and despair before the reality of history."[2]

The schizoid condition of the Christian historian becomes conspicuously evident in the handling of biblical history, and in particular the history of Jesus Christ. Here we see too often that the historian may have learned to confess Jesus Christ as Lord of his own private existential history but not as the Lord of objective world-historical occurrences and movements. Too often his epistemology or methodology falls under the control of secular and naturalistic canons which decree *a priori* what can or cannot happen in history. Because he (our Christian believer who functions as a secular historian) abides by the verdict of positivism, he dispenses with any concern for the reality of history as a whole. As a rule he will limit his method to a phenomenology of history, holding an attitude of reserved agnosticism toward the questions of the reality, truth, meaning, and goal of all history. As an historian he may take cover behind the easy slogan that his job is merely to stick to the facts and not embellish them. To be sure, there are few historians today who are so unsophisticated as to deny operating with presuppositions. When pressed, they will admit that their present interests and perspectives will condition their inquiry and insight. It is generally conceded that there is no such thing as a neutral examination of the facts, but beyond this formal concession there is little clarity or unanimity among historians on how to use the element of subjective interest in historical research. There is always a hidden world view, a hidden religious and moral outlook, in every interpretation of history. The naive historian who claims to exclude himself from his work of writing history will be of the "scissors-and-paste" variety, which R. G. Collingwood rightly ridiculed.[3]

The problem facing the Christian historian is how to let Jesus Christ become effectively the Lord, not only of his private faith, but of his interpretation of history. His conviction that the Christ has appeared in history as Jesus must lead him to interpret history in terms of that event. Any non-christological interpretation of history would have to be anachronistic, proceeding as if the Christ event had not happened, as if he were not the meaning and goal of everyone's history.

The Christian historian can be helped to escape from the prison of scientific historicism by joining the revolution which has occurred among the philosophers themselves. A tradition which includes Burckhardt, Dilthey, Croce, Ortega y Gasset, Collingwood, Jaspers, Heidegger, and Gadamer provides an alternative to the older rationalistic philosophy of history and the newer positivistic historicism. History is neither a philosophy nor a science. It is autonomous; it follows its own laws and principles. The historian is not in search of universal essences or general laws; he has no *a priori* commitment to cram history into what conforms to reason or nature. There are paradoxes, gaps, discontinuities, novelties, instances, individualities, riddles, and mysteries in history which cannot be grasped, as Dilthey acknowledged, in the warp and woof of rational philosophy and natural science. Historians must cease patterning their thinking about history in analogy with the processes of nature. This line of interpretation has an eye to dimensions of ecstasy and transcendence in history. It does not require the historian to read history *sub specie Christi*, but neither does it preclude the possibility of doing so.

Christian faith answers the question of the meaning of history not by a leap out of history but by reference to Jesus Christ. History as the realm of human actions, purposes, values, and forces is the same realm in which God acts redemptively through Jesus Christ. The place of Jesus Christ in this history cannot be defined by fitting him into a preconceived geometrical design. A persistent difficulty in both classic and modern discussions of Christ and history is the tendency to begin with too simple a picture of history. History has been likened to a circle, a spiral, a straight or curved line, a zigzag or wavy line, an ascent or descent, the unwinding of a clock or the denouement of a plot, a swing of the pendulum or the march of Sisyphus, a dialectical triad or an evolutionary monad. But history is too complex a process to be portrayed *more geometrico*, and the Lordship of Christ means that we cannot confine him to a fixed place in history—past, present, or merely future. Therefore, it is entirely appropriate that we preserve a wealth of symbols and concepts to picture Christ's relation to history. He is the alpha and omega, the midpoint and meaning, the center and content, the logos and Lord of history.

The reason the Christian historian must begin and end his interpretation of history with Christ is that he holds no other key to unlock its enigma. He holds no privileged point of view outside of history. Either he remains confused and silent before its nightmarish madness, or he looks for the signs of its meaning *sub specie Christi*. Jesus Christ has entered *wholly* into history without being reducible *only* to it. He is present through his Spirit as the mover of events, yet he is ahead of all as one who has broken the path to the future. Christ is the eschaton of history, gathering up the meanings of time into the eternal unity of the Father. History is the story of promise and fulfillment in Christ, partial fulfillment within time and absolute fulfillment in the eternal future of God.

The meaning of history can be affirmed because the goal of history has been revealed in the midst of time. Eschatology is not a "bundle of secrets" which shall be disclosed in some unknown future. Eschatology is the messianic event of salvation which has happened in history and which in turn creates a missionary history for the proclamation of this event. The history which runs forward from Jesus the Christ is the time for the church to run with the message of salvation to all the nations. That is the fundamental theological meaning of church history.

Eschatology and Christology cannot be separated. The Christian hope for the future is directed always to the person of Christ who has come in history and is perfectly pictured for us in the Scriptures. The future which faith awaits is filled with the presence of Jesus Christ who makes us known to the waiting Father. But the eschatological Christ is none other than the crucified Jew who died like a lousy criminal. And both—the exalted Lord and the humiliated Son of man—are one and the same Jesus Christ who meets us in the gospel and the sacraments.

Christianity is again running a high eschatological fever. Predictions about the future are pouring in, supposedly based on biblical calculations. We cannot emphasize strongly enough that eschatology as the playground of fanatical curiosity holds no interest to us. To be sure, the New Testament does contain many colorful descriptions of the events which cluster around the end of the world. One may naively accept these apocalyptic statements as "colored slides" of historical facts which prophets know will happen in the future. One may take them literally and produce a dogmatics of "last things." But these attempts, reaching back to Tertullian and Hippolytus and fancifully renewed today by Hal Lindsey and other apocalyptists, do not satisfy our curiosity, nor do they provide faith with any solid support and edifying content. They are speculations which deflect the people's attention from the fact of God in Jesus Christ.

Some of the Ritschlians said, "If I weren't a Christian, I'd be an atheist." They meant that Christ is the sole revelation of the reality of God. Without Christ there would be no knowledge of God. We would rather say that apart from Jesus Christ we would not be able to affirm that history has a final and fulfilling meaning. In face of the terrors of the unknown and the horrors of history the Christian can hardly claim any advantage over the existentialist nihilist. His courage and hope are grounded in the victory of meaning he glimpses in the death and resurrection of Jesus. The confession of the nihilist should not be taken at face value. When Jean-Paul Sartre speaks about peering into the abyss of nothingness, nauseated by the emptiness of his own freedom, leaping into a future which only confirms the meaninglessness of the present moment, he is telling us what life looks like from the perspective of the absence of Christ. Could we say that he is an "inverted Christian"? He sees history without eschaton, existence without Christ, *confusio hominum* without *providentia Dei* (Barth).[4]

The Christian shares with all others life under the law of creation, the laws of nature and history. When his contemporaries testify that life has no meaning and there is no salvation in nature and history, that is only a modern way of saying that the law cannot save. The law accuses, terrifies, beats us down, condemns, punishes, kills, drives to hopelessness, despair, and suicide. The law speaks the truth about the human condition apart from the saving gospel.[5] But the law does not speak the ultimate truth—the eschatological word of grace. In light of the gospel the truth of the law is at best penultimately valid.

The conviction that world history has a meaning can be affirmed by those for whom Jesus Christ provides the answer to the enigma of their own history. The biblical paradigm interprets history as the story of salvation, beginning with the experience of liberation from bondage. Israel was created by a salvation event within history. Only on that basis could she later speak of God's purposes for the entire world. Similarly, apart from our personal participation in the salvation of Christ, we cannot broaden the horizon of salvation for the whole of history. The answer to the question of the meaning of my own existence comes prior in the order of knowledge, though not in the order of being, to the question of the meaning of world history. The conviction that "Jesus died for me" is the epistemological prius of the larger belief that "God was in Christ reconciling the *world* unto himself."

History is the story of salvation. We understand history as the material events which God creates as a sacrament of his salvation in Jesus Christ. Therefore, we can no longer view history as a criss-crossing of chance impulses, as an accidental flow of bodies tumbling over the cataract of time to their destruction. Nor can we view it as an immanent structural necessity determined by unalterable powers of fate. We cannot do so because God in his freedom is involved in history to bring it under the power of his rule and to its fulfilling future. Now is the time and here is the place to encounter Jesus Christ as the Lord of history. When the king establishes his kingdom, his subjects are liberated from the tyranny of the usurpers. The Christian has already become a naturalized citizen of the new age. Therefore, he must regard the tyrants of history who oppress the weak and the poor as powers doomed to fade away. People who have accepted the decision of God concerning this world in the death and resurrection of Jesus Christ will not overrate the rulers of this age. With Luther we can still regard history as God's show and the rulers as his agents which keep the show on the road until the glorious epiphany of Jesus Christ to the whole world.

Because history acquires its meaning from Jesus Christ as the history of salvation, we presuppose that history is also penetrated by the powers of sin. Sin and salvation are correlative. Within history the events of sin and salvation occur. An overemphasis on the one aspect to the neglect of the other results in a failure to understand what happened in the cross of Jesus Christ. Here the demonic forces in history concentrated their attack upon the Savior and gained a victory at the expense of their own independent destinies. In the resurrection victory of Jesus over death God vindicated the future of his healing love for this world. World history, therefore, cannot be analyzed merely as a conglomerate of human individuals, institutions, peoples, nations, cultures, customs, ideas, and values. All of these play their part and they may be described phenomenologically—as in the narration of the rising and dying of civilizations by Arnold Toynbee. But if we take our cue from the cross and resurrection of Jesus, we will see history as the battleground of a cosmic conflict between divine and demonic powers. God and

Satan cannot be excluded from the *dramatis personae* of such a spectacle. Every attempt to demythologize this salvation drama will have to
be watched lest in the course of existentially interiorizing the symbols of
Satan and sin, we are left with only shadows of God's work in history.
Worse yet, the cross and resurrection of Jesus also become interiorized
to the point of being mere expressions of the human potential. Then we
are turned in upon our own cold, dark, empty hearts. Then there is no
exit, no salvation. With Mary Magdalene we can only cry, "They have
taken away my Lord, and I do not know where they have laid him"
(John 20:13).

The history of God's work in Israel and Jesus Christ is not separate
from the history of the world which we interpret in economic, political,
and social terms. It is useless to have a redemptive history (*Heilsgeschichte*) which takes place on a different plane than what we ordinarily call world history (*Weltgeschichte*). We cannot abandon this
connection between redemptive history and universal history if the God
who redeems the universe is the same God who created it, and if the
universe which God created is the same one which God redeems. The
symbol of this material connection is the phrase in the Apostles' Creed,
"suffered under Pontius Pilate." The saving suffering is placed in intimate connection with the local mayor of that period. We affirm the
Lordship of Christ not in relation to private religion, but over public
history. There is no dimension of history over which he does not claim
to have dominion. When we confess that he "sitteth on the right hand
of God the Father," we do not mean that he has absented himself from
the affairs of world history as a Lord *emeritus*. Taken literally, in the
manner of Zwingli, this expression would serve to limit his Lordship.
Taken symbolically in Luther's sense this confession emphasizes his
sovereign rulership over all the intermediate events of history between
his parousia in humility and his parousia in glory.

The Christian community as the body of Christ represents the Lordship of Christ in history. This community is authorized and empowered
to proclaim the Lordship of Christ to the world, and thereby to integrate
the world into Christ, as Christ in his incarnation integrated himself with
the world. Even when we cannot see how this is happening in the
events headlined in the morning newspaper—events which seem more to

report the disintegration of world history rather than its integration into Christ—we still live and move and have our being in Christ through faith. As long as faith is faith and not sight, and as long as we let Christ be not only our Lord but *the* Lord, he is the center, meaning, and goal of world history.

Because Christ has made a difference in world history, the church must believe that on the basis of Christ it can also make a difference in the world. It cannot regard Jesus Christ and itself as occupying only invisible spaces outside the interconnected series of events in world history. The old docetism which excluded Christ from existence *in the flesh* has its modern analogue in the tendency to exclude the church from real participation in the turbulent movements of world history. The church is incarnate in the forms and events of history as God in Christ is flesh of our flesh and bone of our bone. As God has acted in Christ, and as Christ acts through his church, so also the church acts for the world. Since it is Christ who is acting when the church acts for the world, Christians are free to believe that things in the world can be changed for the better. Faith in Christ cannot coexist with brooding pessimism or a fatalistic attitude about the future of the world. The fundamental attitude of the church must therefore be hopeful, even when the world's self-witness would seem to justify pessimism as the more realistic posture. The church sees the reality and destiny of the world in light of the promises of God and his actions in Jesus Christ. The church believes that the world is destined to bend its knees before Christ and acknowledge him as the sole Lord of history. The church's pro-world attitude is based on the promise of the gospel that Christ has been appointed to make all things new (Rev. 21:5).

The church is tempted to become impatient on account of the slowness of the coming of the kingdom. Like ancient Israel the church wants to take things into its own hands, redefine the kingdom, and seek to build it by instant techniques. The danger is especially great that Christians, often out of patriotic zeal or revolutionary fervor, will use the name of Christ to endorse their party or program of self-improvement and world betterment. Then Christian belief in the relative alterability of the world on account of Christ is transmuted into a humanistic faith in the perfectibility of the world by means of human accomplishments. But a merely humanistic faith has no way of protecting itself from becoming demonic self-assertiveness.

NO OTHER NAME

If Christ is the center and goal of world history, and if there is salvation only in him and in no one else, how are we to interpret the fact that countless multitudes in other religions and ideologies seem never to have heard the name by which they can be saved? This problem is an essential aspect of eschatological history. If Christ is the eschaton of salvation, what about those people whose histories do not bring them within earshot of the gospel? It is as if an accident of geography or quirk of circumstance should prevent them from an encounter with the name which is above every name. How can Christ be the Lord of history if he does not have the means of making himself universally present in history? His would seem to be a rule by remote control—an absentee Lordship. If Christ is the meaning of history as its universal goal, does not history become meaningless for those people who are not brought into a believing relationship with Jesus Christ?

The problem we have just raised has become a central issue in contemporary Christianity. The issue of salvation through Christ alone has become the focus of discussion in a number of important recent ecumenical meetings. It came up in the World Council of Churches[6] both in Bangkok in 1973 and in Nairobi in 1976. Although these ecumenical meetings were designed mainly to explore the meaning of salvation today in the worldwide struggles for justice, human dignity, and liberation, there were enough evangelical believers present not to allow a disregard for the clear message of the apostolic kerygma that there is salvation for the world through Christ alone, and through no other saving medium.

In the summer of 1974 evangelicals from around the world convened the International Congress on World Evangelization at Lausanne,[7] which underscored the evangelical consensus that preaching the gospel is the primary task of the church and that faith in Christ is the only way of salvation. At this congress there was a group of socially conscious evangelicals who would not let the other side of the truth be forgotten, namely, that social action is part of the fullness of the gospel, and not a mere take-it-or-leave-it afterthought. Besides these ecumenical and evangelical blocs of Western Christians, there is the Roman Catholic Church. Pope Paul VI convened the Synod of Bishops in Rome in the fall of 1974 to deal with the topic, "Evangelization in the Contemporary World." A note of warning was struck by the Pope against both the reduction of the mission of the church to mere social activity and the danger of confusing Christian salvation with one or another aspect of liberation. These three poles of the Christian world in the West continue to grapple with the meaning of salvation in Christ, both with respect to other religious faiths and human development.

A theology of mission must help the church build a bridge between the gospel and the modern world; indeed, we would not need theology at all if it were not for the mission of the gospel to the world. It is one of the vital signs of contemporary Christianity that everywhere people are asking about the essence of the gospel and its missionary relevance to the modern world. But in the process of asking, it is clear that the churches remain confused. The confusion abounds when theologians are called upon to make explicit the truth of the gospel of Jesus Christ in face of the living world religions. This confusion is equaled, of course, by the stuttering response of the church in mission to the world liberation movements.

We cannot afford to have the church go to the world with a split gospel. There are not two kinds of salvation unrelated to each other. We dare not settle for a theology of the gospel which calls on missionaries to sound like mystics in the East and Marxists in the South. We have, instead, the option of equipping ourselves with a holistic theology of the gospel. Our theology of religion and our theology of liberation must both be critically developed in the service of the same name, the same salvation.

We can point to three different theological approaches to the relation of Christianity to other religions.

Ernst Troeltsch has already been dealt with as representing the line of nineteenth-century liberal Protestantism, with its roots in the Enlightenment. Here we can turn to him again as the point of departure of a twentieth-century view which is still in the process of definition and development. Troeltsch pioneered what Paul Tillich called for at the end of his theological career—an interpenetration of systematic theology and the history of religions. Wolfhart Pannenberg is also moving along the same line, although from a vastly different substantive viewpoint.

Troeltsch demanded that systematic theology exchange its dogmatic for an historical way of thinking. The question of the relation between Christianity and other religions cannot be decided by dogmatic prejudice, by prejudgment. Troeltsch complained that Western theologies of world religions have been written by people who have had only a slight acquaintance with the actual data of religious experience and practice enjoyed by persons of other religions. Only by taking into account the actual history of the religions and their interrelationships can the question of the significance of Christianity for other religions be answered. The result is to place Christianity as a religion among the religions, not above them in a category all its own. The historical relativity of Christianity implies that it must abandon its claim to possess the only saving revelation of God to the world. God's revelatory action in Christ is but one slice of the whole loaf of God's revelation in the history of religions, and this Christian portion cannot claim to be the whole of universal revelation and salvation.

This relativistic view of the Christian faith has been updated by John Hick in *God and the Universe of Faiths.* He calls for a "Copernican revolution in theology." Copernicus discovered that the earth revolves around the sun and not the sun around the earth, but according to Hick, we are still mostly pre-Copernican in our theologizing. We think other religions revolve around Christianity and its particular historical revelation, instead of around God and his universal revelation. According to Hick, even Karl Rahner's idea of "anonymous Christianity" does not measure up to the needed Copernican revolution. He dubs it only "another ingenious epicycle to the Old Ptolemaic theology."[8] He defines an epicycle as a theory invented to supplement the old Ptolemaic picture of the world in order to accommodate new knowledge that was beginning to challenge it. We can keep our old theories alive as long as we can invent enough epicycles to take care of the new facts. Let the theory be changed, Hick says, and let us be done with the bother of inventing epicycles. Instead of maintaining the old Catholic dogma about no salvation outside the church or the evangelical belief that salvation is by faith in Christ alone, let us be Copernican and acknowledge that God provides a way of salvation in all religions.

Karl Barth attacked the theology of Troeltsch along with the entire nineteenth-century sweep of things. Barth's concentration on christocentric theology would, in Hick's view, be classified as hopelessly Ptolemaic. Barth's whole theology revolves around the earthly Son, Jesus Christ the Lord, and not around some unearthly deity, as in Hick's Copernican view. In Barth's view God's *exclusive* revelation in Jesus Christ is *inclusive* of the totality of mankind, but not because of religion. His inclusive will unto salvation is solely a matter of grace. In his earlier period Barth defined God in exclusive terms, in absolute distinction from all that is human. In his later development he let God come down to earth, fully embracing and embodying all that is human. Barth accounts for all the religions of the world as much as Hick, but he lets the revelation of God in Christ do all the work. There is nothing left for the religions themselves to do since salvation is through Christ alone, not through Christianity or any of the other religions of the world.

For a theology of mission Barth's position means that there can be only one foundation for the mission of the church. The bridge of mission between the gospel and the world is anchored on the side of the gospel alone, and not in a general revelation of God in the culture or religion of a people. The one revelation of God in Christ excludes every other knowledge of God and every attempt to find a point of contact for the gospel in the world of human experience. Christianity is not the crowning fulfillment of the history of religions. There is no natural theology, no point of contact for grace in nature, for revelation in religion, or for salvation in the structure of human experience.

A third view beyond Troeltsch and Barth is that of Karl Rahner. He has been the dominant figure in rethinking the Catholic theology of mission.[9] With Troeltsch he affirms a saving revelation in other religions and with Barth he clings to the ultimacy of the revelation of God in Christ. This would seem to offer the synthesis we need. In Rahner's view mission is necessary for the church but not essential for salvation. Those who follow Rahner now say there are two ways of salvation according to God's plan. There is the normal way in which a person meets the grace of God in his own religious situation, and there is the special way in which he receives salvation through the gospel of Christ. How these two ways of salvation relate to each other is not explained. Is the missionary really being asked to meet a village Hindu practicing his temple worship as an "anonymous Christian"? Is Christ only a name for the power of salvation enshrined in any man's idol?

We cannot share Rahner's type of universalism. The role of Christ in the salvation of mankind is not worked out on an historical plan. Rather, it is based on an ontological model that restores the old Patristic idea of the *logos asarkos*. Here the *logos* of Greek metaphysics has replaced the word in biblical history in defining the relation between God and the world, between his salvation and the religions of mankind. Nevertheless, the new Catholic theology of the religions is correct in its basic intention of integrating the religions of mankind into the divine plan of salvation. Its universalist thrust would be acceptable if it only were clearly projected as a function of the gospel and its history of promise, rather than as a synergism of two ways of salvation in Christianity and other religions.

Our suspicions of Rahner's theology of mission are confirmed when we look at the implications which some of his disciples derive from it. In an essay, "Guidelines for a New Theology of Mission," William B. Frazier draws the following conclusions from the new view in Catholic theology: (1) The missionary aim of the church is not to bring men the gift of salvation;[10] (2) The grace of Christ always precedes the Christian mission;[11] (3) The world, and not the church, is the focal point of God's saving action.[12] It has also been said that according to this new view, the purpose of the Christian mission is to help Moslems be better Moslems, Hindus better Hindus, humanists better humanists, etc. We have no business calling on people to change their loyalties from one faith to another. This sounds like a radical idea and it will shock many Christians. Actually, however, it must be rejected because it is too conservative for the radicalism of the gospel. It leaves the religious world the way it is; it leaves people to their own religious devices; it settles for the *status quo* in the religious situation of the world. In leaving the religious substance of culture intact, the cultural form of religion remains the same. This is totally ideal for the elite at the top—the priests and the politicians of the establishments—but for the many at the bottom it spells continuing bondage and oppression.

In a systematic theology of mission for today we would like to integrate the chief concerns of Troeltsch, Barth, and Rahner in a comprehensive viewpoint based on a history-oriented eschatology. We must understand the eschatological nature of the gospel in order to affirm the universal scope of its message in history. The task is to take Barth's concern for the christological heart of salvation into a framework defined by eschatological history. The universal future of humanity is linked to the person of Jesus, although he stands as an historical figure in the middle of history. The eschatological future of the world becomes present in the person of Jesus Christ without bringing history to an end. This is the claim of the gospel in a nutshell: the personal future of everyone and the universal future of the world are joined to the eschatological identity of God in the personal life, death, and resurrection of Jesus of Nazareth. We call this the proleptic presence of the eschatological future of God. In the death and resurrection of Jesus we witness the initial breakthrough of the power of God that spells the hope of salvation for the whole of humanity. Jesus has pioneered the future of every person. Salvation is a predicate of the person and work of Christ, not of the cults and idols of any religion as such. We would differ from the Barthian way by placing eschatological salvation into the stream of the unfinished historical process. It is not a *fait accompli* above and beyond history, but is at work in the events of history, transforming it from within. This eschatological salvation is not so much *ganz anders* (totally other), as Barth said, but *ganz änderndes* (totally transforming), as Moltmann holds.

When Troeltsch pointed out the historical relativity of Christianity, this should have come as no great surprise to theologians. Christianity is always being relativized, not merely through its juxtaposition to other religions in history, but even more by its connection with the eschatological revelation of God. All of the church's doctrines and institutions are doubly relativized, both by modern critical-historical consciousness and by the transcendent ground and source of the biblical message. To believe in Jesus is not to stand above the other religions but to place them all beneath the criticism of God's judgment in his cross.

Some have drawn the inference that the historical relativity of Christianity deprives it of any mission to the nations. It can only claim to be meaningful to those within its proper historical orbit. Christianity may be the religion of Europe and the Americas, but why of Africa and Asia? Foreign missions have long enough shared in the pattern of Westernization which the colonial nations foisted upon the rest of the world. If there is to be a universal mission to the nations, it can no longer be linked to the expansionistic drive of the West. That kind of missionary era is now past. On the other hand, if the kingdom of God which Jesus preached is the goal toward which all histories are running, then the message of that kingdom belongs to all the nations of this world.

The church is the representative of the kingdom of God in history— its agent, its anticipation, and its provisional embodiment. With Vatican II we can speak of the church as the *sacramentum mundi*. To us this means that the church is the missionary sacrament of eschatological salvation for the whole world. The gospel of the kingdom places no limits on the church's evangel of hope for the world. The fullness of this salvation is still to come, but its first fruits can already be enjoyed and shared with the whole world.

Does this view open up another way of salvation apart from God's eschatological salvation in Christ? As we have seen, some Roman Catholic theologians are teaching a way of salvation outside of God's self-revelation in the historical Christ of the Bible. They call it the ordinary way of salvation, as over against the extraordinary way which the Scriptures present.[13] Insofar as the intent of this doctrine is to affirm the universality of God's will unto salvation, we would not hesitate to applaud it. In our view, however, the only universalism that can reach far enough to include all people is one that is a predicate of the only gospel of salvation we know. This is a universalism of grace alone on account of Christ alone! In the tradition of Luther and Calvin we deny that we can attain the righteousness of God by our own good works, religious or otherwise. How can the religions of the world produce the quality of true righteousness which we confess not even Christianity can produce? The righteousness of God is a gift of grace, not a product of religion. Religions are among those things that desperately need to be saved. There is only one way of salvation for the whole of mankind and that has been shown to be universally valid and all-inclusive in "the name which is above every name" (Phil. 2:9).

It does not follow that God is absent from the non-Christian religions nor that only Christians will be saved in the end. The gospel is the announcement that God in Christ is drawing all people to himself. The one who is revealed in Christ is at work in all religions as the power of their eternal origin and destiny.[14] Religions are not closed systems. They are all involved in history. They can be sprung open by the gospel on the way to a fulfillment beyond themselves, which they may have already glimpsed, albeit only in a fragmentary way. Religions are not systems of salvation in themselves, but God can use even them to point beyond themselves and toward their own crisis and future redemption in the crucified and risen Lord of history.

THE CHRISTIAN MISSION AND WORLD RELIGIONS

Christianity finds itself today in a situation similar to where it began. It entered the world with only a message that pointed to the universal unity of mankind in the person of Jesus Christ. With only this word and without worldly power Christianity entered into a confusing plurality of cultures and religions, mediating to them a unity that transcended their specific identities. Many religions have gone into the making of Christianity and by the Christian mission have been drawn into the stream of world history.

By a process of historical interaction and interreligious dialogue, a new religious situation is coming into being. If Christians believe the gospel, they will realize that no single religion can contain the *novum* that will be born, not even Christianity. The Bible is a book that belongs to all of humanity, not only to those of Semitic origin. Christ belongs to the nations, not only to Western countries. The gospel is for the world, not only for Christendom. The task of the Christian mission is to witness in word and deed to the universal unity of the whole of reality in Jesus Christ. This is not a message against the religions but for them.

What is the proper approach of Christians to people of other religious faiths? This has become a central issue in both Protestant and Catholic circles. Paul Tillich in Protestant theology and Raimundo Panikkar in Catholic theology have stimulated new insights into the relation of Christian faith to world religions. Their spirit of openness to the revelation of God in the world religions has encouraged a series of studies and dialogues sponsored by the World Council of Churches. The great world religions are referred to in more affirmative language as "living faiths."[15] The older exclusivistic attitude that roots in Pietism and modern evangelicalism is for the moment out of favor. Yet few are attracted to the old liberal idea as a workable hypothesis, namely, that all religions share a common substance and are equally valid ways of salvation.

Shortly before his death Paul Tillich delivered a lecture entitled, "The Significance of the History of Religions for the Systematic Theologian,"[16] which could serve as a point of departure for rethinking a Christian theology of the religions. Tillich rejects two attitudes that make the theological task all too easy. The first is a theological rejection of the religions, on the ground that they are false, man-made efforts to reach God which contain no revelation at all. This position is identified with simplistic Barthianism. A second attitude is the secularistic dismissal of religion as passé in a world in which modern man has outgrown his adolescent myths about God. Tillich attributed this position to the death-of-God theology.

To Tillich a fuller affirmation of the religions is based on certain assumptions. First, there is divine revelation in all religions. Second, this revelation is always received by man in a limited and distorted way. Third, in order to discern what has revelatory significance it is necessary to subject the history of religions to criticism. Fourth, there may be one event which unifies the revelatory experiences within the religions. From the point of view of Christianity, this one event is the appearance of the New Being in Jesus as the Christ. Fifth, religion and culture are not separate phenomena, but are dimensionally related to each other.

On the basis of these assumptions, a theology of the history of religions can definitely liberate mission for a more open and inquiring attitude toward elements of value in non-Christian religions. Not everything has to be written off as hopelessly pagan. The New Testament itself, as the Old Testament writings before, clothed divine revelation and salvation in symbols and myths drawn from the religious traditions of the Mediterranean area. The figure of Jesus was placed in the context of a long preparation in religious history. We learn from this that God's revelation is always incarnate in concrete religious expressions. In Tillich's view, the whole history of revelation in the religions is a preparation for what he calls "the Religion of the Concrete Spirit."[17] This religion cannot be identified with any particular religion, not even with Christianity as a religion. The inner aim of the history of religions is to be realized in such a Religion of the Concrete Spirit, yet not in the sense that is wholly future. We could say that in, with, and under all the religions there are authentic elements that point to this Religion of the Concrete Spirit, the criterion of discernment being the religions' fight against the demonic. Sometimes this fight takes mystical form, at other times a prophetic one, and even the secular critique of religion can be seen as a struggle against the demonic perversions of religion.

All of these ideas must seem extremely speculative for the missionary troops on the frontline of the interreligious encounter. In fact, however, they can be very useful in guiding Christians who find themselves in dialogue with people of other faiths. According to the New Testament Jesus is the liberator from the demonic powers of darkness, death, and destruction. He is Victor. Therefore, the power of Jesus is not alien to the forces—however partial—already at work in other religions fighting the demonic elements. Jesus is the Lord of lords. Tillich sees in the cross the message of victory over every demonic claim. Such a christological approach does not lead to an exclusivism which simply condemns all religions *in toto*, but offers a criterion for discerning whatever is true, good, and worthy of inclusion in every religious synthesis.

The christological claim is binding on Christian participation in dialogue with other religions. Yet, very different attitudes have been promoted and justified on the basis of Christology. The most common attitude in the missionary movement has been exclusivistic: only a few are thought to attain the state of salvation. The evangelical theology of mission, for example, has consistently rejected belief in universal salvation, a rejection ratified at the Lausanne congress of evangelicals in 1974. The ostensible reason is biblical fidelity; evangelicals seem less aware of their roots in Pietism. There is more backing for a gospel of universal hope in the Bible than evangelical pietism has been willing to adopt in its system of salvation. Pietism is radically person-centered:

the eye of the evangelist is always on the individual, with a view to motivating personal conversion and ongoing growth in spiritual life. Only individuals *qua* individuals can be saved. Only born-again Christians will enter into everlasting fellowship with the Father in heaven; all the rest will be damned and thrown into the lake of eternal fire (Rev. 19:20). What a person does or does not decide now seems absolutely binding on God in the day of judgment.

Exclusivism has produced its own consequences for the Christian mission. Individuals who have experienced regeneration form an exclusive fellowship—an *ecclesiola in ecclesia*. These fellowships—existing often alongside the established church which is seen as a mixed body of true believers and hypocrites—often have become mission societies, sending missionaries to foreign lands to salvage as many individuals as possible from eternal shipwreck. In the new land natives who become converts often separate themselves from their people and culture and enter into the missionary colony of the saved. This evangelical pietistic spirituality is world-negating—the world is the field of mission, but not itself the thing to be saved. The person and not the world in all its social, political, and cultural manifestations is the exclusive target of the gospel.

Understandably this exclusivistic view of mission has triggered a reaction of the opposite kind in which elements of universalism are integrated into Christology to promote an inclusive vision of the salvation of mankind. Since World War II we have witnessed a revolution in mission thinking, the guiding slogan of which has been "openness to the world." Among Roman Catholics Vatican II marks the turning point away from its traditional exclusivism; among Protestants the new turn can be traced to Dietrich Bonhoeffer's theology of the world. The church has been stimulated to a new openness to the world, to discover the mighty acts of God not only in the past records of holy history, but in the whole non-Christian world of today, including both its modern secular as well as its traditional religious aspects. There is salvation outside the church, at least outside the visible organized church. Some would go so far as to say there is salvation apart from Christ, at least apart from his concrete identity in the historical Jesus.

There are two variants of this world-centered redefinition of the

Christian mission. On the one side are the advocates of secular Christianity. They think of salvation as the promotion of humanity in radically secular terms. In the sixties it seemed that Christianity would be deluged by the secular spirit, and theology became a sort of scholasticism, devoting itself to hair-splitting distinctions between such terms as *secular, secularity, secularism,* and *secularization.* On the other side are those who seek apologetic links with the religious renaissance. Eastern mysticism is welcomed as a fresh breeze on the barren plains of Western secularism, and salvation is defined purely in religious terms. Salvation exists everywhere outside the church, leading one cynic to say, "The only question is whether there is salvation inside the church."

A church holding a world-centered theology of mission will cross frontiers expecting to discover experiences of salvation wherever it goes.

The Spirit has not failed to bestow his gifts on people in other religions. Christ is already present, albeit hiddenly and anonymously, in the world, as the source of its light and life, prior to the church's arrival on the scene.

What, then, is the point of the church's mission if the grace of salvation is possible without it? The church becomes a sign of salvation, at best bringing to light what is hiddenly present, proclaiming and interpreting what God is doing everywhere, discerning the power of salvation at work wherever it can be found in the world. The missionary aim of the church is then not to get new members, nor to expand the church by crowding more of the world inside its walls. Rather, the aim of the church's mission is to focus its energies on making the world more alive to its own potential, to make human life more human, to assist persons in other religions to share more fully the mystery of salvation present within them, thus to make Jews better Jews, Hindus better Hindus, humanists better humanists, etc. The idea of conversion is turned completely around from its meaning in evangelical exclusivism. Instead of converting people to Christianity, we hear of converting the church to the world. Instead of inviting people to see what God is doing in the church for their salvation, Christians are asked to behold what God is doing in the world for its fulfillment. This is to take seriously the world as the object of God's saving action, and to make the church a people serving the world.

If the evangelical theology of mission has the merit of stressing the aspect of particularity in Christianity, the modern ecumenical approach has sought to recover the aspect of universality. Both aspects are rooted in the New Testament. The interest in particularity does justice to the role of concrete faith and the historical Jesus. The motif of universality seeks to broaden the significance of Christ and God's love for the world, so that nothing lies outside the scope of his saving power and eschatological glory.

We must seek a christological solution to the problem of balancing the particular and universal aspects of salvation. Jesus Christ is the point where history has become pregnant with eschatological meaning and the world with universal hope. Any attempt to solve the problem by purely person-centered or world-centered approaches leads always to either a false exclusivism or a false universalism. Whereas exclusivism sees that Christ is the center of salvation, it limits the circumference of his saving meaning to a particular kind of subjective psychological response to him. On the other hand, a world-centered universalism sees the cosmic circumference of Christ's meaning, but relies on the world's own natural structures—religious or secular—to mediate the universal grace of God. The centering of salvation exclusively in Christ is surrendered to give the world its share of the action.

A position closer to the truth is one which views the church as embodying *both* particular and universal aspects. The concrete church of history bears a message of salvation for the whole world. The church is both apostolic and catholic, rooted in the historical vocation of the apostles and expanding in the direction of every culture and society. This is in principle true, but in practice the church has promoted a self-centered view of mission and salvation. Strategies for planting the church (*plantatio ecclesiae*) and church growth (cf. McGavran's mission theory) can lead to a triumphalist view of the church's role in the salvation of mankind. Persons tend to be looked upon as potential members. The world is seen as raw material for the church's development as it seeks to broaden its sphere of influence or control. The flaw in this view is the virtual identification of the kingdom of God with the church, as though the signs of its coming are limited to what the church is doing in the world.

We can scarcely forget that the church-centered view of mission gave a special impetus to the expansionistic drives of Western colonialism. The idea of spreading the blessings of Christian civilization to primitive folk in heathen lands became closely linked to the missionary aim of making everybody in the world Christian and producing church members in good standing. Gospel and culture became fused into one reality. The World Mission Conference in Edinburgh in 1910 spoke too confidently of Christianizing the world "in this generation." The Western missionary, as Martin Kähler warned, was in grave danger of becoming a propagandist for civilization in the name of the gospel, bent on making carbon copy Christians or, worse yet, a Xerox copy of his own denomination. On the mission field the church tended to become an enclave of Western Christianity, a mini *corpus christianum*, a colony of aliens helping to alienate the natives from their own ways of being and behaving.

The classical saying that "outside the church there is no salvation" was appropriated by and in turn nourished this triumphalist church-centric view of the Christian mission. It led to the most hideous excesses of the missionary movement, the harvest of which we are now reaping in the form of a backlash against mission as a tool of Western imperialism. Another interpretation of this classical formula is possible: there is no salvation apart from that which God has given to the world through Christ and his church. The church does not possess all the salvation there is, but there is no other salvation for the world than the one it has witnessed in the Christ event and partially embodies in its message and mission. A better formulation might be that outside the salvation to which the church points there is no lasting hope for humankind. Better yet, since the formula has been subjected to so much misunderstanding, it would perhaps be wisest simply to give it up and reconceive the matter in christocentric terms.

THE GOSPEL OF UNIVERSAL HOPE

The church has a message for the whole world. Its universality does not lie in its own social organization but in its message concerning God's final revelation in Jesus Christ. This christological claim to finality does not necessarily breed intolerance toward other religions. No

promise is given in the New Testament that the church will displace the
world religions. It is under no obligation to impose its own doctrines
and structures on other religious communities. The universality of the
Christian message is not negated by the fact of religious pluralism in the
world. The attribute of universality is part of the church's eschatological orientation, not a predicate of its own historical existence. Even
where the church is destined to be a minority in a non-Christian culture,
she still represents the way, the truth, and the life for all. The recognition of the right of other religions to exist does not invalidate the universal promise to the nations.

The church has had to revise some of its dreams about converting the
world to Christ. It is no longer plausible to believe that the church will
score big victories on secular or religious fronts. This sobering thought
should lead to modesty and humility, but it should not be interpreted to
allow the gospel to surrender the claim to universal truth and validity.
Theologians have no basis for taking the attitude that Christians are
only a little flock with no particular mandate to change the world.

As the colonialistic mission of Constantinian Christianity is laid to
rest, the church does not find itself off the hook in respect to the universal mission of the kingdom. Only the Lord of the church can retire it
from its field of service in world history. No matter how poor and
powerless the church may become in worldly terms as the representative
of the universal gospel of God's kingdom, it is still the place where the
Lord and Savior of mankind engages the world in a search for whole
meaning and a fulfilling future, an engagement which may take the
form of an angry denunciation of a political tyrant à la John the Baptist
or the more genteel form of interreligious dialogue. The church is the
place where the question of ultimate human concern is to be raised and
answered. Any limitation of these aspects of universality, ultimacy, and
finality, makes the church a religious sect existing in radical contradiction to its own apostolic constitution.

The question we must finally face is how the world can hope to
receive the salvation offered by God through Christ. What kind of
knowledge is needed for the world to attain salvation? What kind of
faith? It is clear that the church has been preaching the gospel for two
thousand years and yet the world as a whole does not believe in the

Christ of God, Jesus of Nazareth. Some predictions even suggest that Christianity will lose the numbers game and become increasingly a minority of the world's population. Christianity enjoys majority status only where the birth rate is under control but precisely there—in Western nations—mass defections from church ranks are taking place. The picture is not so bright if we look at statistical probabilities. So how is it possible to hope for the world if salvation is limited to the few who truly believe in Jesus Christ?

There are well-known attempts to solve this problem. It has been argued that saving knowledge of God can be had apart from Christ (John Hick), or that Christ can be known apart from the Christian gospel (Raimundo Panikkar),[18] or that there is a latent church in the world religions without any manifest connection with the historical revelation in Jesus Christ (Paul Tillich). Each of these positions results in whittling away at the foundations of the Christian conviction that Christ and his church are God's links of salvation to the world he loves. It is God himself who has elected particular means of grace to reach the universal end of salvation. This is an inherent aspect of the scandal of the gospel, the offence of the cross. Theological speculation has tried to build wider bridges for God to attain the goal of universality, but it is a blow to the Christian mission when speculation soars into a lofty universalism at the expense of the particularity of the historical media of salvation. Christianity must accept and hold resolutely to the paradox that God will attain the universal goal of salvation through the particular means he has chosen, though it appears to reason that an unbridgeable gulf exists between means and end.

The Christian hope for the destiny of the world rests solely on the gospel of Christ and not on the religions of the world. Trust in the gospel generates the hope that the eschatological future which arrives through Christ will one day—the day of the Lord—bring a fulfillment to the world unmatched by past and present experience. We believe, therefore, that no person's individual history possesses ultimacy in itself and that the final judgment is not determined by merits of achievement —religious or otherwise—but solely according to the boundless mercy and omnipotent love of God. To be sure, now is the time of decision when people are to be confronted by the preaching of Christ. But Jesus

Christ is Lord also over the times when peoples and nations will encounter his Lordship. We do not look for another name of salvation. By faith we exist in the tension of the gap, hoping against hope in him who will reveal the new reality of the world, hoping against hope that the end of the world will be its universal fulfillment and not total annihilation outside the living God.

It is because Jesus Christ is the only Savior of mankind that we can hope for a universal restitution (*anakephalaiosis tōn pantōn*) inclusive of people who worship at shrines where the name of Jesus is not yet known. As the Lord of history Jesus Christ is also Lord of the world's religions. We can believe that providentially God is at work in the many religious traditions, drawing them together into a unity being forged for mankind in Christ. There is an eschatological dimension to the belief that the one straight and narrow way of salvation is the point of convergence for all the streams of human religion. There is also an historical dimension to this belief. It takes the form of specific action in the name of Jesus—communicating words of eternal life and doing works of love and freedom. These eschatological and missiological brackets on the problem of the one salvation and the many religions rule out any theory by which each and every religion generates its own valid way of salvation. To be sure, God has not left himself without witnesses anywhere in the world, but the same Scripture makes equally clear that the ultimate truth to which these witnesses point is incarnate in the person of Jesus.

It is important to add that the confession of Jesus as Lord and Savior of mankind should not lead to a narrow focus on Christianity as the final form of faith in him. The finality of Jesus Christ cannot be appropriated by those who bear his name. Their traditions are relative, limited, provisional, and open to change. Christianity as we know it is already a syncretism of many religious ideas, symbols, rites, and practices which have been taken captive and baptized into the name of Christ Jesus. The same thing is going on today. Christianity is free to take on new forms in Africa and Asia because Jesus is to be crowned as Lord also in non-Western sectors of human experience. We stand on the threshold of a new chapter in world history, when Christians in Africa and hopefully also in Asia will present us with confessional, liturgical, and organizational forms vastly different from those we have known in the last two thousand years of church history.

NOTES

1. The material in this section of the chapter represents an abridgement and revision of my article, "Christ Today: The Lord of History," *Lutheran World* (July, 1963), Vol. X, No. 3, 257–266.

2. *The Philosophy of History in Our Time*, Hans Meyerhoff ed., (New York: Doubleday, 1959), p. 23.

3. R. G. Collingwood, *The Idea of History* (New York: Oxford University Press, 1956), p. 257.

4. Karl Barth, *Church Dogmatics* (Edinburgh: T. & T. Clark, 1962), IV/3/2. pp. 693 ff.

5. The Smalcald Articles, Part III, Article II. *The Book of Concord*, Theodore Tappert ed., (Philadelphia: Fortress, 1959).

6. See *Bangkok Assembly 1973*, Minutes and Report of the Assembly of the Commission on World Mission and Evangelism of the World Council of Churches, December 31, 1972 and January 9–12, 1973.

7. See the comprehensive volume of papers and responses coming out of the Lausanne Congress on World Evangelization, *Let the Earth Hear His Voice*, J. D. Douglas ed., (Minneapolis: World Wide Publications, 1975).

8. John Hick, *God and the Universe of Faiths* (New York: Macmillan, 1973), p. 128.

9. Karl Rahner's most important writings on the Christian mission and world religions are scattered in various volumes of his *Theological Investigations* (Baltimore: Helicon), especially Volumes V, VI, VIII, & IX.

10. William B. Frazier, "Guidelines for a New Theology of Mission," *Mission Trends, No. 1*, Gerald H. Anderson and Thomas F. Stransky eds., (Grand Rapids: Eerdmans, 1974), p. 29.

11. *Ibid.*, p. 31.

12. *Ibid.*, p. 34.

13. H. R. Schlette, *Colloquium salutis—Christen und Nichtchristen heute* (Cologne, 1965); also "Einige Thesen zum Selbstverständnis der Theologie angesichts der Religionen," *Gott in Welt II*, J. B. Metz ed., (Freiburg: Herder, 1964), pp. 306–316.

14. Wolfhart Pannenberg, "Toward a Theology of the History of Religions," *Basic Questions in Theology*, Vol. II (Philadelphia: Fortress, 1971), pp. 65–118.

15. S. J. Samartha, ed., *Dialogue with Men of Living Faiths* (Geneva, 1971).

16. Paul Tillich, "The Significance of the History of Religions for the Systematic Theologian," *The Future of Religions* (New York: Harper & Row, 1966).

17. *Ibid.*, p. 87.

18. Raimundo Panikkar, *The Unknown Christ of Hinduism* (London: Darton, Longman & Todd, 1964).

5

THE FUTURE OF CHRISTIANITY IN AMERICA

THE CRISIS IN AMERICA'S FAITH

If the kingdom of God was ever meant to have a mission in world history, the hour has struck in America for a revelation of its power of judgment and renewal. The state of the union rests heavily on the right response to the challenge of the future. Eschatological faith has a mission in America to renew the vision of the kingdom of God, not only as eternal bliss for souls alone, but as the source of hope for these times of trouble.

The scenarios of the future are mostly pessimistic. These ultra-modern times are already shaping up like the last times of which Jesus spoke in the "little apocalypse" of Mark 13. There he listed the signs of the endtime: wars and rumors of wars, nation against nation, kingdom against kingdom, earthquakes and famines, trials and tribulations; children will rise up against parents, Christians will be hated, false Christs and false prophets will show signs and wonders; even the sun and the moon will get dark, the stars will fall from heaven, and the powers in the heavens will be shaken.

How is that picture so different from the present, with its crimes of violence, genocide, urban decay, drug abuse, mass starvation, nuclear proliferation, religious wars, race riots, political torture, problems for the aged, the poor, and the mentally ill, population explosion, and environmental pollution? People speak apocalyptically about the approaching end of the world and books written on the subject—all in the name of the Bible—are among the best sellers.

Eschatological faith is alive in America today, having been revived in face of the impending collapse of our civilization. Since Spengler more and more people are prophesying the decline of the West, including America, with almost chiliastic fervor. The question we are facing is whether eschatological faith will function merely as a private consolation for the few who dream of eternity ahead, or whether it can also work retroactively upon these times of trouble as a dynamic force in constructing public images of hope.   The dualism of biblical eschatology is not two-faced, presenting a private face of salvation for individuals and a public face of damnation for groups, be they nations, cultures, societies, or religions.   The one God of the Bible is the Lord of history, whose promises to Israel have been shared with all the nations, who enters into social and cultural processes to shape the public images which define meanings and goals.   The old saying is true for both groups and individuals, "Tell me your vision of the future, and I will tell you what you are."   If America's vision of the future is disintegrating or degenerating, the scenarios of the future will give nothing to shoot for, but will remain only a blowup of present troubles in various combinations.   The shadows of these troubled times are cast forward to darken the horizon of our future.   "Where there is no vision, the people perish."[1]

Is there a mission of eschatological faith for America today?   One temptation for Christians is to escape into heaven with their faith, leaving the world behind.   Another is to run into the world and play the game by its rules, reserving faith for a realm of privatude.   Both extremes are ways of transforming the two-dimensional reality of the kingdom of God in history into a one-dimensionality of either the future or the present.   The former leads to sectarian other-worldliness, the latter to a humanistic this-worldliness.   In either case the mission of Christian hope for the future of America is aborted, since the dynamics of the world and the kingdom of God are forced to run along separate tracks.

Perhaps we ought to state our thesis as an ultimatum.   Unless there arises a strong counterattack from the side of the eschatological faith which gave birth to this nation and shaped its covenant, our culture will continue its headlong rush to breakup and decline.   Like small fishing boats we have drifted too far away from the mother ship, and have to find our way back for fresh supplies.   Can anyone doubt that the real sickness of American culture today is a loss of faith in our mission and destiny under the kingdom of God?   We cannot take for granted that the pendulum of faith will swing back in time to place our civilization once again on the course marked for it by the chart and compass of its founding promises. Only faith in the unbroken validity of the promise of our origins can check the claws of the beast that are tearing the fabric of our present. But is it not unrealistic to hope that the elements of meaning and destiny, of judgment and grace, can come to life again in the body of our nation?

There is this ancient wisdom: he who does not believe in miracles is not a realist. What else is the Christian mission in America all about? Christianity is essentially a future-oriented mission and a matrix of hope for the world. When the hopes of other people begin to wane and they want to quit, Christians are going to stay in the game until God blows the whistle for them to stop. Reinhold Niebuhr wrote in *Moral Man and Immoral Society*, "There is a millennial hope in every vital religion. . . . Whenever religion concerns itself with the problems of society, it always gives birth to some kind of millennial hope, from the perspective of which present social realities are convicted of inadequacy, and courage is maintained to continue in the effort to redeem society of injustice."[2] His brother, H. Richard Niebuhr, whether the major or the minor of the two American prophets we cannot say, a few years later traced the development of American eschatological faith in his book, *The Kingdom of God in America*. Neither of the Niebuhrs is proposing a single-cause theory of the socio-cultural dynamics in the American experience. Neither are we. But as H. Richard Niebuhr demonstrated, the kingdom of God has been the dominant idea in American Christianity and only by reference to it can we interpret the American dream and explain the effect of Christianity on American culture.

There is creativity and tragedy in the story of the kingdom of God in America. The vision of America as God's empire was deeply rooted in the Puritan faith in the sovereignty of God. Deep in our bones we have carried the sense of divine mission in America. The world's hope is somehow linked to the success of God's "grand experiment" (Horace Bushnell) in this part of the world. Josiah Strong articulated the common faith when he said: "God has two hands. Not only is he preparing in our civilization the die with which to stamp the nations, but by . . .

'the timing of providence' he is preparing mankind to receive our impress."[3]

The early Puritans had no doubt that the kingdom of God was God's, the living power of his rule in the entire human world, and certainly not a utopia built on the moral purity of human hearts and social planning. H. Richard Niebuhr traces from that point the many religious and social experiments under the swaying power of God's rule. He shows how various Christian groups tried to realize the reign of Christ in their lives and communities, how they looked for the coming of the kingdom as the power of the end rushing to meet them, bringing great peril to the souls of men and also great promise for a millennium of liberty, peace, and justice. The rule of Christ was meant for both personal and social spheres.

"If the seventeenth was the century of the sovereignty and the eighteenth the time of the kingdom of Christ, the nineteenth may be called the period of the coming kingdom."[4] Then came the tragedy, the fall of the kingdom of God into the hands of a secularized and nationalistic civil religion increasingly alienated from Christian eschatology. Therewith it lost the power to sustain the elements of cleansing judgment, great hopefulness, and positive images of a future anchored in a transcendent goal. Unguarded optimism came to rest on a humanistic belief in progress. The coming kingdom became evolutionary utopianism. The belief of American Christians in being chosen for a new experiment of God in world history turned into the dogmas of divine favoritism, of national superiority, of being the best nation on earth, and of being right in every war. The Social Gospel movement, right as it was in extending the benefits of salvation to the social realm, lost its grip on the original eschatological character of the kingdom of God. H. Richard Niebuhr wrote the classical inscription on the tombstone of liberalism's eschatology. He said, "The idea of the coming kingdom was robbed of its dialectical element. . . . A God without wrath brought men without sin into a kingdom without judgment through the ministrations of a Christ without a cross."[5]

Does the fall of eschatology in Protestant liberalism represent the end of the kingdom's history in America? It is my conviction that we may find symbols of healing and reconstruction in the biblical roots of American experience, and that other symbols must be rejected as invasions of foreign influence. As a body must tap its own resources to win its way back to health, so must we open our eyes to the eschatological vision of the coming kingdom which has been the dynamic power of movement in American history. Not this vision itself but the blurring of our eyesight accounts for its distortion into an ideology of national arrogance, economic exploitation, and military expansionism. The heritage of eschatology more clearly than any humanistic ideology—liberal, utopian, or revolutionary—brings down the judgment of God against such tendencies. America is in a grave crisis today not because of its pursuit of the ways of God's kingdom in history, but because of its compulsion to identify the kingdom with its own empire and naturalize the deity as one of its citizens.

CIVIL RELIGION: CAN IT BE SAVED?

The question is whether eschatological faith can be born again as the driving force in American culture. There can be no Christian theology of history without eschatology, and thus no believable meaning in the course of human events. When the future of God's judgment and redemption no longer beckons on the spiritual horizon of this nation's people, the keynote struck by the decadent minds of many Western intellectuals who sound the meaninglessness of human existence in the meanderings of world history works its demoralizing effect in the soul of America, especially in the younger generation. Civil religion does not have the spiritual and moral power to build a mighty fortress against the waves of iconoclastic prophecy that wash away the foundations of hope in American experience. For civil religion is scarcely more than a secularized humanistic residue of the kingdom of God, absolving God of his promises and leaving the nation to guide its own destiny by power politics. When the transcendent point of reference has vanished, we no longer seek God's will or purpose, no longer move toward an end or goal, no longer live by hope and expectation. Civil religion in America, devitalized by the secularization of the kingdom of God, is like a lame man trying to lead a blind man. The nation has lost its vision of God's mission, which holds it accountable to his coming kingdom and its righteousness, spelling justice among men, peace in the world, and freedom for every person.

Robert Bellah has prophesied that the hope of salvation lies in American civil religion. Whatever may have caused him to temper his view in *The Broken Covenant*, written between Vietnam and Watergate and no doubt touched by the mood of the disenchanted liberal of that period, his most influential and most quoted essay is on "Civil Religion in America." Others have tried to build on its optimistic assessment of the redemptive potential of civil religion. He defines it as religion in its public dimension expressed in a set of beliefs, symbols, and rituals.[6] The God of this civil religion owes some of his most characteristic attributes to what we have called eschatological faith. As once God concerned himself with Israel of old amidst the nations, so now he is doing an analogous thing in America as a model for the world. Bellah points out rightly that history may be conceived as emancipation from the Egypt of European bondage to the promised land in America. Like Israel, America acquired her sacred scriptures—the Declaration of Independence and the Constitution—and possessed a mission beyond America to the whole world. Bellah also acknowledges that the New Testament themes of death and sacrifice, rebirth and reconciliation, have also been worked into the religious consciousness of the nation, especially by Lincoln. As evidence for the fact that civil religion is still very much alive in America he points to Kennedy's "new frontier" and Johnson's "great society." These are positive notes. On the negative side, Bellah acknowledges that this civil religion has pleaded for many of the wrong causes. Bellah speaks of "dangers of distortion",[7] having in mind the treatment of minorities, fear of nonconformism, the legitimation of imperialistic adventures, and alliances with oppressive governments in the name of freedom. Just when he waxes most pessimistic, however, he takes hold of the Ariadne thread of civil religion to guide us through the labyrinth of these times of trouble.

Can civil religion do the job? Bellah says it will have to possess certain components which now are extremely weak. The first is belief in a transcendent God; the second, a clear note of judgment; and the third, a universal vision of America in a community of nations. Bellah envisions "a new civil religion of the world."[8] Such a new religion would be the outcome, he says, of "the eschatological hope of American civil religion from the beginning."[9]

It is a strange spectacle to see how a thinker of Bellah's stature can dress up civil religion in such new clothes without realizing that what he is describing is just plain Christianity. The Christian theology of the kingdom of God in history is equipped precisely with those components which Bellah finds missing in present-day civil religion—transcendence, judgment, and universality. These are the elements which have been flattened out by the process of secularization, for which the churches deserve a share of blame. At rock bottom the mission to which Bellah calls civil religion is simply impossible of fulfillment until it has first returned home like the prodigal son.

What can we expect for cultural renewal from a rebirth of eschatological faith? Utopian humanism cannot point to a power beyond the human condition which can create something new and better. We must reawaken—if it is not too late—the awareness of God's future dormant in the vitalities of the American Dream.[10] We have absolutely no confidence in a new religion or in a culture without religion. What is wrong in looking for a new generation of founding fathers and mothers, to write a new declaration of interdependence for America amidst the nations, led by tough-minded visionaries who know how to make their dreams come true? It is impossible to believe that America needs anything more urgently than a rebirth of meaning and mission, direction and goal, value and virtue. Certainly it cannot be more wealth and resources, more power and guns, more science and technology. Let us stipulate some of the factors involved in a rebirth of eschatological faith in American culture.

First of all, we must learn from the Old Testament that monotheistic faith has to do with the very nature and meaning of the entire course of history, including the future. Faith in one God means to believe in the power of his rule over the whole of history. Only a part of his plan has been realized. For this reason eschatology is an essential implication of faith in one God, anchoring the power of his rule in the final future of all reality. A god who had no power over the future and the final goal of all things would be no God at all.

Second, we must learn from history that eschatology has already exerted a powerful influence on the course of events, because it is not the human projection of mere wishful thinking but the divine foundation of assured expectation. Its psychological trademark is fervent faith, not half-hearted longing. Even the long-range images of biblical eschatology that cluster around the end of history such as resurrection, judgment, new heaven, and new earth, eternal life and the like, have short-term effects in these times before the last. They have to do with the way a person builds his own house and lives in it. Eschatology is dynamically related to history.

Third, after a lifetime on the study of history, Arnold Toynbee was able to distinguish the Christian eschatological way of thinking and feeling about temporal existence and cultural life from all the others:[11] archaism, which dreams about restoring a golden age in the past; futurism, a utopianism that simply jumps into the darkness of an unknown time or place; and escapism, which detaches itself from this world. Christian eschatological future transcends this world without ceasing to include its ongoing transformation. The recovery of the Christian eschatology of history is the last chance for our culture, if it is not to give up the ghost to any of the other three philosophies of history.

Fourth, eschatological faith at work in culture can strengthen the will to resist evil in all its subtle and overt forms. Eschatology is the source of both the prophetic denunciation of evil and the spiritual drive to relativize every situation that claims to be part of an absolute order. Eschatology challenges the vested interests of the present order in the name of an alternative order with a higher right to be. It keeps alive hope's mission to change what needs to be changed and tirelessly opposes every power which stubbornly resists.

Fifth, eschatology expands our sense of reality. A culture with an eschatological vision at its heart is protected from vulgar materialism and spiritless positivism—two serious cultural diseases which underlie all the rest.[12] The kingdom of God does not exist, yet it is as real as God. This invisible reality of God and his coming kingdom, the norm and goal of all that exists, forbids us from confusing this world with the kingdom of God and from believing that this world is the totality of the really real. This eschatology can protect us from the social myths that polarize humanity into two absolutely irreconcilable classes. It will succumb neither to a utopia of the upward-striving class which believes that the kingdom of God will arrive with the revolutionary realization of its interest, nor to an ideology of the ruling class which believes that the transcendent values of universal freedom and justice are mere visions not meant to come true in time.

Sixth, eschatology keeps the social myths by which people live from becoming demonic. Millions of human beings have been killed in our century by the lethal force of the social myth of national socialism, fascism, and both Soviet and Maoist communism. It is silly to believe that modern man, with all his science and technology, has advanced beyond the stage of mythical consciousness. The Christian myth nails all rival myths to the cross of demythologizing by the hammer of divine judgment. If this did not occur the social myths would become inflated to pseudo-eschatology, calling for ultimate human sacrifice in the interest of less than ultimate values. That is the mark of the demonic in society.

AMERICA: QUO VADIS?

Eschatological faith would become sterile if there were no way for it to cross-fertilize with the dominant cultural forms of the present. Christian eschatology must in some way link up with secular futurology, or simply be classed among things like crystal-gazing, fortune-telling, and astrological chart-reading.

There is no doubt that America has been ultradynamically oriented to the future. But what are its objectives? We have been going forward at breakneck speed, but to what destination? Alvin Toffler has spoken of "future shock." America has become strong on means, weak on ends. If we are going to move the train rapidly away from the station of the *status quo*, would it not make sense if we had a clear picture of the *terminus ad quem*? Otherwise it seems we are putting up with a lot of poison, rats, riots, slums, poverty, traffic jams, pollution, crime, inflation, taxes, and all kinds of political corruption pretty much for nothing. Where are we going, and why? *Quo vadis*, America?

I would propose that high on the church's list of priorities in mission should be to engage our culture in a conversation concerning our common future. What does the church have to contribute to a dialogue about the future of our future? We know from Columbus' letters to the royal households of Portugal and Spain, begging for money for his explorations, that a certain eschatological picture of the future was a recurrent theme in that correspondence. The argument was that since the end of the world was just around the corner, it would be terribly important to convert as many heathen as possible so they too could go to heaven. And thus the new world began. Our conversation with the power elites of today could not repeat Columbus' argument, nor could we expect to reap the same success as he enjoyed in his fund-raising campaign. Yet it is about the future that we must hold a dialogue. Can there be a cross-pollination between biblical symbols of the eschatological future and secular models of the historical future, to the end of shaping the very future of our future? If we do not mould the future into the shape of man, the future will shape man into the mould of a monster.

We know now that the main powers of the world—military, industrial, and governmental—are funding think tanks staffed by expert scientific and technological forecasters. Their secrets—privy to a select group of insiders—are translated into policies, plans, and programs that affect the quality of life for every man, woman, and child on earth, plus all the fowl of the air, the fish of the sea, and everything that creeps upon the earth. The mentality of these people, exemplified by Herman Kahn, is shaped by science, not by con-science. Their explorations of the future manipulate people in the present in order to keep the future open to the few but closed to the many: there is just not enough of a future for all, so let us make sure we get ours.

The church has no expertise to contribute to such future research, insofar as that research is dependent on cybernetics and computers, mathematical statistics and probability theory. We are in no position to refute the polls or dispute the trends. People are in fact inclined to look fatalistically upon these scientific and technological prognostications. *Que çera, çera*—whatever will be will be. This only reinforces the trend which allows more and more of the power to fall into the hands of an elite few.

So where does the church fit in? Fatalism is totally incompatible with Christian belief in the freedom of God to act in history. Nor has the power of God been transferred to the new technology. The future is a book sealed with seven seals, and no one in heaven or on earth can read it except the Lamb who sits upon the throne. So the first word is this: people with big ideas about the future, dressed in language about exponential growth, explosion, revolution, and systematic change, do not really know the future. Their scenarios are blown-up versions of the present. Our first task is to debunk the myth that the future has finally come under man's control.

The second task of the church is to represent the human quotient in every dialogue about the future. This is a normative mission-oriented function that must be strengthened wherever scientific futurology is taken seriously. Mission-oriented futurology counts on the relative alterability of the trends out of which scientific extrapolations are made. The uppermost question is, What values and goals shall we pursue? The quality of the future we aim for cannot be negotiated on a purely scientific basis. We count either on people who have what Plato called the "divine spark" in their souls, or we prepare for a future without a human face—beyond freedom and dignity, to use B. F. Skinner's words. Good old-fashioned American know-how, magnified by science and technology, will not give us a liveable future, unless the softer gifts of intuition, imagination, fantasy, and faith share in forming a picture of the know-what. There is a yawning hiatus between our modern knowledge of how to do something and what to do it for. At this level we are dealing with theological and ethical, or at least religious and humanistic, issues. The church's vision of the eschatological future of God's world is not only for souls in another world, but is to be used to swell the knowledge of what ought to be changed in this world and to buttress the courage to stick to the task despite the odds. We have to pick up the thread of argument with all futurists wherever the theme of human dignity is involved.[13]

The third task of the church is to keep people sensitive to the lines of suffering in the human face. It is not enough to instill in us a future-consciousness alone, for such a consciousness when not inspired by love for the individual person is potentially destructive of the human race. The church is to remember that its passion for the future can never race ahead of the neighbor in need, lest it be like the priest passing by on the other side. No image of a collective good, however utopian, is acceptable if the way to such a future is attained by grinding the faces of the poor.

How can the church penetrate the rock-hard realities of the present with its soft-hearted ideals about human dignity and new community? Its vision carries far beyond socialism and capitalism as we meet them today. It keeps alive a highly-charged tension between actual and ideal reality. But first the church must begin to believe in and live from its own promises for the future, becoming something more than a "rough average" of what people in general hope for. There are signs that the church is aging. Its own dominant images seem hardly attracting to the younger generation. If there is a famine of hope in the church, there will not be much of a banquet in the culture of America's future.

TOWARD A CHRISTIAN INTERPRETATION OF AMERICA

The bicentennial of our nation, in 1976, has brought forth an outpouring of books and statements on how to relate Christianity to America. Many of these doubt the validity of eschatology, while others deny its viability in the construction of America. We are faced with a situation in which something else than eschatology is most commonly used to shape the Christian mission in the American context. Further, operative eschatological faith is usually relegated to the private sphere, leaving the public domain to the powers that be. There are, to be sure, signs that a new breed of evangelicals is emerging, ready to explore ways to liberate their biblically-oriented faith for a wider mission in the field of culture and the world of politics. Without denying that the history of salvation has an eye on the supernatural destiny of the world, some are beginning to see that the interim is a time in which God has his eye on the salvation of world history. The politicizing of the great potential of evangelical consciousness in American religion is a promising sign for the future.

A Christian interpretation of America can only be discovered by those who struggle within the orbit of its colossal power. For this reason the task cannot be left to Americans alone, or to those who live within its borders. The power of the American empire is now universal. The culture of which it is the leading example is also universal. Not a single literate person in the world is outside the orbit of America's influence.   Therefore, every world citizen has a perfect right to make his statement about the meaning of America.   As members of an international movement called Christianity we have brothers and sisters in many lands who can help us interpret the reality to which we as Americans have become so thoroughly reduced, that we can scarcely project a horizon broad enough to embrace the experience of the victims of our own power.   The silence of the churches during the war in Vietnam is an example that should never be forgotten of how many Christians in America let the horizon of the state function as their own.   The passionate outcries of fellow Christians abroad were dismissed as anti-American prejudice.   The international scope of Christian identity should empower every Christian to offer a double reading of his nation's meaning in history, first, in light of his own shared identity with his fellow citizens, and second, in light of the broader perspective that comes from solidarity with members of the same mission in other countries.

What happens when there is a conflict between these two readings of America in the world?   There is such a conflict today.   It lies in America's self-interest to continue to dominate the nations of the Third World and keep them in a state of dependency, even while feeding them slogans about democracy, development, and interdependence.   We need to control the raw materials and the markets abroad to maintain our affluence at home.   Contrariwise, the interest of the Third World is to liberate itself from the vicious cycle of dominance and dependence, from every instrument of neocolonialism and imperialism.   Where shall the Christian who is also an American stand in this conflict?   Those who imagine this to be less than a conflict bordering on revolutionary explosiveness have no awareness of the magnitude of misery and anger in those regions chosen for exploitation in the interest of foreign advantages.

The Christian who is also an American will reject outright an ethic which justifies his nation's imperialistic actions on the basis of self-interest.   There are limits to self-interest beyond which the nation becomes a tool of the Anti-Christ in history.   The Christian knows that the kingdom of God does not grow in accordance with his nation's own expansionistic desires.   Rather, his own nation is a battlefield for the universal kingdom and its demonic antagonists. The church is to disclose the judgment of God over those demonic forces running wild in the nation, lest she herself join the state in becoming a tool of the Anti-Christ.[14]

The Anti-Christ is a superpower of oppression and domination in history. America is not the Anti-Christ, neither is the church the kingdom of God. But the church is to represent the kingdom of God under the conditions of the social, political, economic, and cultural systems, and thus do battle against the demonic forces that would hand the nation over to the Anti-Christ.

The church as the representative of the kingdom of God in history must be in a position to use eschatological criteria to discern and disclose the demonic forces in America today. Her vision of the future kingdom is one in which every group identity based on land or language or culture or religion is gathered up in a multi-dimensional solidarity of universal peace. Organizations such as the United Nations and the World Council of Churches, as ambiguous as they happen to be, are partial down payments on the eschatological fulfillment in store for mankind. Every system, therefore, which lives from competition between groups, destroying the peace for which they are destined is demonic. The church's vision of the future also includes a picture of humanity in harmony with nature. Every system, therefore, which places profits above concern for both people and the earth to which human life is linked is demonic.

The category of the demonic applies to capitalistic society on the condition that as a system it inherently and systematically creates an opposition, not only subjectively but objectively, between those who own the means of production and those who are dependent on them.[15]
The distinction between classes is one of capitalism's structural elements, working itself out in the economy as well as in such other areas of life as where one lives, what schools one can attend, and what medical care one can afford. We believe that what Paul Tillich wrote in the 1930s is still valid in our day: "Religious socialism calls the capitalistic system demonic, on the one hand, because of the union of creative and destructive powers present in it; on the other hand, because of the

inevitability of the class struggle independent of subjective morality and piety. The effect of the capitalist system upon society and upon every individual in it takes the typical form of 'possession'; its character is demonic."[16]

A moralistic appeal for Americans to become more Christian or more humanitarian is of little value. What is needed, rather, is a disclosure of the real powers that grip the souls of the American people, the powers that make them feel and think the way they do. Something more than a change in attitudes is needed, something more than a religious conversion. The forms and conditions of our life must change. The structure of capitalism must go. The meaning of democracy must be expanded to mean not only the right to vote but the right to work for a decent living under conditions of human dignity. A system that either requires or causes unemployment is intolerable.

The kingdom of God does not give the church a blueprint for the perfect society, but it does inspire a vision for a more meaningful society than the one we have. It can lift up human and communal values that embarrass the powers that work death and destruction in society and in the lives of people. It can show how the promises of God are the materials from which to fashion a dream of universal peace and justice, freedom, equality, love, and solidarity. It can also call us into the missionary service which as a sign of the power and presence of the kingdom in our midst can make that dream come true.

Our criticism of American capitalism may appear like we are beating a dead horse since, in fact, pure capitalism does not exist. What is known as capitalism in America today is a hollow mockery of that nineteenth-century theory which had all the marks of a utopian vision. According to the theory there was a "hidden hand" of providence bringing about harmony between the self-interest of capitalists and the general interest of the people. "What is good for General Motors is good for America," said former G.M. president Charles Wilson. The capitalist faith included the belief that competing self-interests, if left to work freely (*laissez faire*) in the public market, would automatically lead to progress and prosperity for all. As though echoing the Apostle Paul, "The sufferings of this present time are not worth comparing with the glory that is to be revealed to us" (Rom. 8:18), the capitalist creed could regard the evils it generated—misery, poverty, and unemployment —as nothing compared to the coming paradise of plenty it promised for everybody.

Today even the captains of big business do not share the tenets of that capitalist creed. They may pay it lip service, as do the politicians, but in fact the free enterprise system is marked by state interventionism, protected by regulations, and cushioned by subsidies. The bold entrepreneur who was willing to risk everything in the free market has been replaced by the salaried pragmatist who is more interested in steady growth and security.

Nothing is to be gained, however, by jumping out of the frying pan of capitalism into the fire of socialism. The socialist vision, like the capitalist faith, has given way to technical managers and pragmatic politics, making its own hallowed phrases about equality and solidarity sound hollow. The politics of capitalism and socialism begin to look more like each other as they attempt to work out realistic solutions to problems in a framework of world peace. On both sides, too, a small clique in charge of the decision-making apparatus, whether of industry or government, steers a vast army of anonymous members who are convinced their own votes do not count.

Christianity has no reason to bless one *system*, capitalism or socialism, in the present world situation. It cannot give its assent to a particular economic theory or propose specific solutions to political problems. The essential thing is not to lose sight of its own vision of a meaningful society. A particular nation may have to make its own decision between capitalism or socialism as systems of economic and social organization; the church is not called on to make that decision. The international diaspora of Christians serves the nations best by being true to its own vision and bearing it witness through words and deeds. What is this vision? We have taken the position that we cannot accept the vision of capitalism, because it inherently, and not only by chance failure of its implementation, creates a division in society between owners and workers, producers and consumers, profits and needs. The golden calf of money becomes the god of a system which works for profits, not for people. It is a system which inherently, and not occasionally, demands competition and not cooperation. The result is that the big fish gobble up the little fish, and some of these little fish are the family farms, small businesses, village shops, and useful trades. For a Christian to accept the capitalist vision is to give blanket endorsement to social Darwinism—the survival of the fittest. The fittest are the biggest, those who must successfully compete in their own interests, basically to make profits and only incidentally to serve people. Such a vision appears realistic; it takes into account what theology has called the "old Adam" and proposes to build an entire social system on natural drives. It is the institutionalization of the original sin of egoistic existence. A vision inspired by the "new Adam" is accordingly dismissed as utopian.

Biblical eschatology has sown the seeds for a utopian vision of man in society. The Christian vision of the future is the grandfather of utopian socialism. We are not referring to the societies of the East which have opted for the socialist system, all of which are marked by contradictions of basic elements of the socialist vision. The socialist vision is a dream always in the process of being realized in history, a quest for the new man in a new society. At no time can we point to an existing society and cry "Eureka!" That would entail a demonic exchange of one finite epoch in history for the final kingdom.

We will conclude this chapter with a brief sketch of the Christian social vision, trying to reduce it to basic concepts.

The Christian vision of a meaningful society is dynamically oriented to the future as the realm of the new. Israel moved from the wilderness to the promised land, from exile to homecoming, from captivity to the coming of the Messiah, and thus it could always envision a future radically broken from the existing state of affairs.

The Christian social vision is a passionate plea for a new order of relations in which the poor will have plenty and the oppressed will rule. A reversal of the realities that now hold sway will take place, so that the last will be first and the first will be last.

This social vision says that there is a time for sowing and a time for reaping. A minority of creative persons will continue to sow the seeds of truth even though only God knows when and if they will ever ripen. We know that visionaries of past times have made possible many of the realities we now take for granted. Even Gerald Ford defended programs which Norman Thomas once was ridiculed for having dreamed up.

The meaning of being human lies in the freedom to work for the common good. Human dignity can be achieved only in the context of equality and mutual respect among people. For this reason it must rebel against an individualistic idea of freedom which drives each man to live for himself lest he fall under the slavery of another.

Christian socialism expresses itself by being radically prophetic rather than by pragmatically seeking an accommodation with existing realities. It finds breathing room for being human in the action of protesting against the mechanistic, materialistic, and mass-minded programming of people. Its struggle is against the powers and principalities, not merely against the flesh and blood of day-to-day politics. History shows that when socialists gain power, they lose their vision. The road to socialism is closer to the kingdom than its result when transformed into a concrete system.

The vision of a liberated society must be kept alive by a multi-national community that resists as a temptation of the devil the will to seize power. The church is just such a community, and for this reason it will not consecrate a particular political party or program of economic development. Such a community must straddle all the parties so that its members may be drawn from the left and the right and the middle, thus finding a fellowship of reconciliation in the midst of conflicts.

This vision of a meaningful society is only one aspect of the community of the endtime. As a religious vision it points to a sacred, sacramental dimension of meaning both for the person and the world in the life of the world to come. There is a religious substance of faith, hope, and love that is directed not only to the development of mankind for its present good, but points finally to God as the source of all good. Vision of God is finally the source of social vision, keeping it conscious of the provisionality of its own forms and therefore free from falling under the axe of its own criticism.

NOTES

1. Proverbs 29:18.
2. Reinhold Niebuhr, *Moral Man and Immoral Society* (New York: Charles Scribner's Sons, 1932), pp. 60–61.
3. Quoted by S. E. Mead, "From Denominationalism to Americanism," *Journal of Religion* (January, 1956), 14.
4. H. R. Niebuhr, *The Kingdom of God in America* (New York: Harper & Brothers, 1937), p. 150.
5. *Ibid.*, p. 193.
6. Robert Bellah, "Civil Religion in America," *Religion in America*, William G. McLoughlin and Robert Bellah eds., (Boston: Houghton Mifflin Co., 1968), p. 6.
7. *Ibid.*, p. 16.
8. *Ibid.*, p. 20.
9. *Ibid.*
10. Robert Benne and Philip Hefner make a positive assessment of this possibility in *Defining America* (Philadelphia: Fortress, 1974). The authors call for sacrificial attitudes and openness to the future to regenerate the American Dream. Their book is marked by greater confidence in the redemptive potential of civil religion than we can share. In our interpretation Christian faith and civil religion are as different as Adam and Eve before and after the fall. The one is by nature a corruption of the other. The "religion" of civil religion is the enemy of faith, as the old Adam is the enemy of the new Man in Christ.
11. Arnold Toynbee, *A Study of History*, the authorized abridgement of Volumes I–VI by D. C. Somervell (New York: Oxford University Press, 1947), pp. 431–433.
12. See how this thesis has been elaborated in detail by F. L. Polak, *The Image of the Future*, Volumes I & II (New York: Oceana Publications, 1961).
13. Ted Peters has correlated and contrasted different perspectives on the future, taking the stance of an historico-eschatological hermeneutic similar to our own in *Futures—Human and Divine* (John Knox, 1976).
14. See Jacques Ellul, *The New Demons* (New York: Seabury, 1975).
15. Except for William R. Coats' enthusiastic endorsement of "socialism" in *God in Public, Political Theology Beyond Niebuhr* (Grand Rapids: Eerdmans, 1974), I agree with his critique of the capitalistic system.
16. Paul Tillich, *Political Expectation* (New York: Harper & Row, 1971), p. 50.

6

THE LIBERATION OF MISSION AND THE MISSION OF LIBERATION

THE CHALLENGE OF LIBERATION THEOLOGY

The current rise of liberation theology provides an occasion to rethink the Christian mission from new perspectives. Numerous personal observations of the role of this theology in the Third World—Asia, Africa, and Latin America—lead to the conclusion that this theology is not merely the latest of the fads. The theology of liberation is not to be dismissed as a consumer item of fad-hungry theologues in the United States and Europe. I have found it alive and doing well, especially in those areas where colonial theologies are fading away. It is a theology natural to a people who live close to the Bible and appropriate its stories as paradigms for their own struggles for freedom. Certain members of the academic establishment dismiss liberation theology as a product of a few superstars now taking their turn at being used by the media to popularize a fad. Such establishment theologians do not understand that the theologies imported during the era of missionary colonialism are unable to take root in situations where the struggle for freedom is the guiding theme of a mass movement. Looking from afar, they do not realize that liberation is not the brain child of the academic superstructure, but the emerging reflection of a people engaged in the praxis of liberation.

Liberation theologians feel that for the first time they are doing their *own* theology out of their *own* situation.[1] Heretofore they have worked with a second-hand theology. Like all other manufactured goods, theologies bore the stamp "Made in Germany," in England, Sweden, Spain, Italy, or America. Missionaries put the Bible into the hands of Third World peoples in their own native tongues, but the accompanying theologies came prepackaged from foreign countries. Since every theology bears the marks of its own cultural situation, alienation was built into

139

the missionary churches' process of teaching theology. Converts to Christianity often became alienated from their own society while learning the dogmatics of a foreign religion.

Liberation theology always starts with an analysis of the concrete situation. Thus, it operates with a built-in corrective against the traditional imposition of ready-made theologies from the outside. It is understandable that Western theologians with their long history of world preeminence would look upon liberation theologians as brash upstarts who have a lot yet to learn. Home-grown liberation theology will in the future provide stiff competition for the more sophisticated theologies produced by the academic establishment in Europe and America.

Liberation theology reflects the fighting interests of groups whose causes have not been lifted high in our standard theological texts. Professional theologians, whether in universities or seminaries, have not been at the forefront of the struggles of the Third World, Blacks, Chicanos, women, students, the world proletariat, the poor, the oppressed, and other marginated people. When liberation theologians speak of the theology of their oppressors, there is little doubt whom they mean. They are speaking about *us*. Whites wrote theology for Blacks; men wrote theology for women; adults wrote theology for children; Europeans for Africans, Spaniards for Indians, intellectuals for peasants; colonialists for the colonized; the rich for the poor. Some produced, others consumed. Liberation theology is convinced that each group out of its own situation has to write theology for itself, and opposes those who seek to control others by doing it for them.

Liberation theology can claim the distinction of being the most truly ecumenical theology. Traditional confessional differences presuppose a firm attachment to the past. Since most dogmatic disagreements were produced by rival factions in the age of Christendom, they tend to perpetuate themselves mainly where such a mentality still exists. In the glossary of liberation theology, *Christendom* is another word for "domination." The doctrines which Christendom produced lose their binding authority when Christian faith is born anew in the struggles for liberation. The authority of the past has to yield to the critical needs of the present and the imperatives of tomorrow. This is not to say that liberationists function without a memory principle as though the past were sealed off. The point is that memory must serve the call to freedom and the mission of liberation today, and thus people coming from the most diverse denominational backgrounds find themselves united in the liberation struggles. In Latin America, for example, liberation theologians come from the evangelical right (Orlando Costas), the Protestant middle (José Miguez-Bonino), and the Catholic left (Gustavo Gutierrez and Juan Luis Segundo). Divided by where they come from, united by where they are, they are able to think and act in solidarity with all who turn the good fight of faith to the advantage of the poor and the oppressed.

Liberation theology is a thorn in the flesh of "North Atlantic theology" because it draws not only from the atheistic writings of Feuerbach, Nietzsche, Freud, and Sartre, but also from the revolutionary sources of Marx, Lenin, Mao, and Marcuse, thus giving rise to attacks on the alliance of classical liberal academic theology with the elitist classes of society and their socio-economic self-interests. *Liberal* theology has been linked to the very structures which keep the oppression going. It can hardly be expected to bite the hand that feeds it. Thus, liberation theology does not understand itself as a variant of liberal theology. It is as likely to draw its recruits from evangelicals steeped in fundamentalism and biblicism. Theologians who defend to their dying day the right of theology to clothe itself in Platonist, Aristotelian, Cartesian, Kantian, Heideggerian, or Whiteheadian categories should not be so inconsistent as to deny liberation theologians the freedom to do the same in Marxist or Maoist thought forms. What scandalizes is not atheism—theologians have gotten used to that even in their own ranks. Rather, offence is taken at the revolutionary thrust which cuts into the marrow of self-interest, calling for concrete change, instead of merely flitting along at the level of abstract ideas.[2]

Liberation theology has been wrongly advertised by people who stress its novelty. There is something new, to be sure, but not so much *substantively* new. Its sources and symbols have been around for a long time. They are as old as the Old Testament,[3] most of them anyhow. What is new is its way of doing theology, its contextual concreteness, and its option for praxis as the aim of theology, rather than the rationalistic goal of clear and distinct ideas. Because it is a theology oriented to the concrete involvement of the church in society, calling for dramatic changes for the sake of the little people at the bottom, its implications for the church's mission in the world are many and far-reaching.

Gustavo Gutierrez speaks perhaps for all liberation theologians when he states: "The theology of liberation offers us not so much a new theme for reflection as a *new way* of making theology. Theology as critical reflection on historical praxis is thus a liberating theology."[4] Liberation theologians are usually so busy making theology that they scarcely reflect on the issues of method in theology, yet it is at the methodological level that their own claim to originality lies. What is this new way of doing theology? Critical reflection on historical praxis is the key phrase. The data that count in theology are not exclusively, or even primarily, derived from Scripture and tradition. They arise historically in the concrete particularities of what is going on. This notion of the priority of praxis has a close affinity with the pattern of the primitive Christian community in which theology grew out of the missionary proclamation of the church in concrete encounter with the world. Martin Kähler's phrase, "mission was the mother of Christian theology," accents the same priority of practical action over theoretical reflection. Theological theory is empty without missionary praxis.

Liberation theology thus aims to speak concretely not abstractly, prophetically not speculatively, objectively not subjectively, politically not mystically, polemically not neutrally. Truth is not so much an attribute of ideas as a mark of action. The biblical notion of "doing the truth" is preferred to an idealistic model of getting human thoughts on earth to match a heaven of eternal ideas. The truth of a theory cannot be known and elaborated in advance, only to be applied at a later time. Truth emerges in language that reflects a community's engagement in the liberating transformation of history. In the course of such liberating praxis we find the clues to what God is doing in the world.

Liberation theology agrees with Pannenberg's dictum that "history is the most comprehensive horizon of Christian theology."[5] It begins with concrete historical experience and then raises from within the issues which call for theological reflection. It begins with social analysis and then proceeds to ask about the meaning of the gospel and the church's mission. Thus, in books that claim to be theological we find ourselves working through tons of sociology, politics, economics, and modern history. We have to stretch our working vocabulary beyond words like historicity, existential, self-understanding, ontic, and kerygmatic to include a new series of expressions like conscientization, multinational corporations, developmentalism, ideology, imperialism, and the like. Strange as it may seem, the method itself should not be unfamiliar. It conforms to the notion of the priority of law over gospel in traditional Lutheran hermeneutics. This was even a claim that Bultmann made for his own existentialist interpretation of the New Testament: existentialist philosophy functions as law in the clarification of the kerygma in terms meaningful to modern man. So now liberation theologians can claim that their use of Marxist socio-political analysis does not replace the gospel with an ideology, but clears the path for theological reflection in a strict sense.

Liberation theology is suspicious of the claim to neutrality of the liberal theological establishment. Liberation theologies debunk the myth that any theology can be above politics or stand beyond partisanship. Some liberation theologians consciously adopt the Marxist analysis of society, and charge their liberal opponents with using the mask of theological neutrality to hide their own hidden alliance with the ideological biases of the dominant classes. Juan Luis Segundo entitled his five-volume work *A Theology for Artisans of a New Humanity*. He might have substituted the word *partisans* for "artisans," since he is openly committed to a liberating praxis that aims to socialize the means of production, overcome the classist society, and educate the masses to take part in the political process that determines the conditions of their life.

Scripture is not the only text of the theology of liberation. In a real sense the present situation is the primary text and point of reference. Yet, this theology has opened up new channels of biblical interpretation. It is generally the heir of the historical interpretation of the Bible and carries forward the recent European creation of a political hermeneutic of the biblical message, albeit a political hermeneutic which is applied more radically and consistently. The Bible is viewed basically as a document reporting the public and political activity of God the liberator.

Its hermeneutic is political in a revolutionary sense. The politics of God from exodus to the resurrection effectively denounce the church's alliance with structures of economic, social, and political oppression. The Bible is not a classic of human religion, but a subversive document of divine revolution in history. The Bible has been called "the bad conscience of the church." Its message disturbs a complacent and world-conforming church. Biblical paradigms show that God has himself entered into solidarity with the poor and the oppressed, placing his chosen people under obligation to do the same. Fighting for the kingdom of God in history means taking sides with those who struggle for freedom, justice, and peace. The fundamental datum of Scripture is that Yahweh, the Father of Jesus Christ, is the one who hears the cries of the afflicted and works to overcome their taskmasters. The story of the Exodus is the prime model of how God acts in history, and if we were to choose one text that enshrines the mind of God, it would be the Magnificat of Mary, the Mother of Jesus:

> He has put down the mighty from their thrones,
>> exalted those of low degree;
> He has filled the hungry with good things,
>> and the rich he has sent empty away. (Luke 1:52–53)

Liberation theology takes the concrete political imagery of the Bible and resists every attempt to neutralize it into an abstract spiritualization of the meaning of salvation.

The theology of liberation is monistic in its view of history. It cannot see the church as having any mission to build a separate history, but rather as leading the way in expressing and exemplifying the one meaning of the one history. The mission of the church is inescapably tied to historical struggles for liberation. Salvation does not occur elsewhere than in and through this struggle. The Protestant Reformers rejected the dualism between nature and supernature as inadequate for the depiction of man's standing before God in solidarity with the whole creation. Such a dualism, however, has in fact been kept alive in Neo-Orthodoxy with its distinction between history and suprahistory or between *Heilsgeschichte* and *Weltgeschichte*. This rejection of two histories in favor of a unitary view of history, however, is not unique to liberation theology. Both Pannenberg and Moltmann have rejected the split-level theory of history in which God's acts were relegated to a special realm of redemptive history. With the wall of partition falling between sacred and secular history, liberation theologians perceive God's acts in the world today in line with the events the Bible reports, acts which are not miracles of the past to be immortalized in a trophy case called Holy Scripture. The idea that God acted in biblical times, but acts no longer like that, is a deistic residue which still clings to theologies that claim to be biblical. Since liberation theology stresses not only what God did, but also what he does in the present, it is appropriate to call this a "theology of the signs of the times." It is prophetic theology, strong on proclamations of judgment and hope. It dares to speak for God in the midst of world-historical affairs.

In looking to politics for its chief metaphors, the theology of liberation tends to break with the classical alliance of theology with metaphysics. Definitions of God that speak ontologically are set aside in favor of the historical language of politics.[6] The reason modern theology ended up in so much empty talk about the "death of God" is that it abandoned the *polis* as the arena in which to speak of God. Theology pulled its God language into the sphere of personal and private life, letting it die the death of irrelevance. The strategy of liberation theology is to recover the meaning of God language within the context of history. Any separation between the revelation of God and the history of mankind must be overcome. This means that theological reflection and political praxis need to be unified at the point where the idea of God occurs in the first place. It is not the case that politics is what man does, while theology reflects on what God does elsewhere, say, on the inside of a person's private life, in mystical experience. One will not find much of metaphysics and mysticism in the writings of liberation theologians.

Liberation theology offers an interpretation of history guided by what Paulo Freire calls "a generative theme." He contends: "I consider the fundamental theme of our epoch to be that of domination—which implies its opposite, the theme of liberation, as the objective to be achieved."[7] *Liberation* is here another word for salvation.

The generative theme of the Reformation was justification. That was the thing to be achieved by the sinful man.   Luther discovered the paradox that the sinner, not the righteous person, is justified before God on account of the righteousness of Christ. For liberation theology, sin is more usually thought of as a predicate of a social situation characterized by structural distortions such as classism, racism, sexism, and capitalism.   Sin is conceived in sweeping social categories.   The Roman Catholic bishops of South America issued a document at Medillin, Columbia, in which they spoke of the social situation itself as sin.[8]   Sin is not a purely personal relationship.   Instead, sin is historicized; the depth dimension in the vertical line between God and man is fleshed out in the horizontal language of sociology, politics, and economics. Gutierrez says, "But in the liberation approach sin is not considered as an individual, private, or merely interior reality—asserted just enough to necessitate a 'spiritual' redemption which does not challenge the order in which we live.   Sin is regarded as a social, historical fact."[9]   The place to look for sin is in "oppressive structures, in the exploitation of man by man, in the domination and slavery of peoples, races, and social classes."[10]   This approach is sometimes referred to (pejoratively) as the horizontalization of the human predicament.   It deals not so much with the roots of sin (original sin) which go deep into the infrastructure of each person and all humanity, but rather with the branches of sin in the objective structures of society.

The preaching of salvation is meant, strictly correlatively, to fit the shape of sin.   Therapy is meant to fit the diagnosis.   Since the shape of sin in liberation theology is basically social and horizontal, the answer to this universal situation of misery and tyranny is the historico-political process of liberation.   The goal of liberation is an abundant life for all and release from the conditions which deprive people of freedom, justice, and dignity.

The preaching of salvation in traditional Christian missions is often severely criticized because it links the soul to an other-worldly heaven, ignoring the mundane conditions of life to which a person is temporarily bound with his body.   Such a dualistic approach plays into the hands of those whose advantages are served by the present system.   Liberation theology wants to break the back of a dualism which permits salvation to shoot off into an abstract world of souls above and beyond, leaving this concrete world in the hands of those who govern it to their own advantage.

The challenge of liberation theology to the traditional evangelical concept of the church's mission is nowhere more keenly felt than in its thoroughgoing rejection of the doctrine of the two kingdoms. This doctrine allows God two ways of working in the world, one through the gospel of salvation and the other through the law of creation at work everywhere in the world. The church has placed its mission in the service of the right hand of God. It claims no special charisma, though it cannot exempt itself, with regard to the public works of the left hand of God. This gives rise to the language of prioritization: the priority of the church in mission, so it goes, is to preach the gospel, administer the sacraments, to care for the brother in need, to evangelize, and render diaconal service. Whatever else the church does in the world occurs through its individual members in the secular vocations. The official church, licensed by the State, is free to practice its religion so long as it remains politically neutral or institutionally cooperative. Liberation theology, however, has unmasked this nominally a-political posture of Christianity as a hidden ideology of reaction, leaving the world free for the demons of oppression to keep all power in their filthy hands.

Liberation theology's analysis of the church's actual role in society shows that none of its actions are void of social and political content. The church may pretend to be nonpolitical, but this is only true in the narrowest sense of "party politics." The church may not tell its members to vote Republican or Democratic, but even its claim of having primarily a spiritual function carries with it the political consequence of shoring up the established order by taking the heat off. The church that washes its hands of political responsibility is like Pilate washing his hands at the trial of Jesus. He presumed to be guiltless while mass hysteria condemned an innocent man to death. Many churches in modern times have tried to walk the tight rope of neutrality between their gospel mission and political involvement. More often than not they have fallen to the side of political conservatism, rarely to the side of social change and revolution. Hence, many view the church as standing on the side of the oppressors. Its transcendent gospel offers people an abstract salvation for an abstract soul, quite out of sight of the concrete powers that move the world.

We have declared ourselves decidedly on the side of liberation theology insofar as it makes the social and political dimension of human activity integral to the church's faith and mission. The political aspect of life is not a gratuitous dimension of faith reserved for a handful of Christians who like to get involved. "The church is wholly mission," only if mission is defined in terms of a *critical eschatology* that calls the church to serve as an institution of social criticism. The only way to make the mission of the church credible in the context of racism, sexism, and classism is to turn the eschatological hope of heaven into a revolutionary transformation of society.

Liberation theology is relatively optimistic about the capacity of the church to effect humanizing changes in the social situation. Therefore, it calls upon the church to use its political power against existing power structures. Many of the leaders of liberation theology come from a Roman Catholic tradition, and thus speak from intimate experience of the church's ungodly alliance with the powers that be. The model they criticize so devastatingly is that of Christendom. It strips away the church's traditional presumption of a political innocence which has negotiated privileges for itself out of reach of the common people.

SALVATION AS LIBERATION

Liberation theology contributes much to any rethinking of the Christian mission in world history. Its concept of salvation is radically incarnational. The Word has become history; the Spirit has become somatic life; the eschatological future is becoming present. Salvation is not only something to wait for but something to be done. Salvation in history is legitimately translated into liberating action. Salvation is addressed to man as a whole, body and soul.

The old body-soul dualism lies behind much of the resistance of evangelicals to liberation theology. Evangelicals say they are interested in "eternal remedies" and not mere "temporary palliatives" as offered by the social gospel of yesterday and the political gospel of today. A theologian such as Peter Beyerhaus, a leading spokesman of the evangelical theology of mission, makes a clear distinction between the gospel of salvation and the goal of humanization.[11] Such a dichotomy is nourished by a hidden dualism that separates aspects of human and historical reality that belong together. It leads to a sub-biblical affirmation of eternal salvation for souls to the disparagement of the establishment of peace, the struggle for justice, and the promotion of human welfare.

Behind such a splitting of salvation is that creeping spiritualism that places the human body at the bottom rung of the ladder of reality. There is no such thing as the salvation of souls apart from the body. Salvation is historical, social, and somatic. We play out the drama of God's salvation in our bodies and nowhere else.[12] The criterion for the presence of salvation is not spiritual ecstasy but somatic wholeness. Many Christians still suffer from a gnostic hangover, thinking of Christianity as a religion which wings souls into an other-worldly communion with God.

The gospel according to liberation theology calls Christians to the front lines of history to practice the good news of liberation for all mankind, beginning with the poor and the oppressed. The secular dimensions of common human experience cannot be excluded from the universal gospel. Nothing in heaven or on earth, nothing in history or nature, no private individual or social group, no experience of the nation or of the church lies beyond the scope of the liberating gospel of Jesus Christ. Religious individualism and other-worldly salvation are both to be rejected on account of the incarnational flow of divine salvation and its universal breadth in human affairs.

Having affirmed the relevance of liberation theology for rethinking the Christian mission in our time, we would nevertheless be untrue to our own historico-eschatological perspective if we did not issue a caveat in the spirit of constructive criticism. Those who have accepted the death of the old forms and eagerly look for new forms of mission are frequently vulnerable to the limitations of a new and challenging viewpoint. The basic limitation is an overreaction against the traditional supernatural concept of salvation and an other-worldly orientation of the church's mission. In a holistic theology of the kingdom of God it should be possible to give expression both to the depth dimension of the evangelical idea of salvation as well as to the breadth dimension of the historical concern for liberation. The unitary view of history which most liberation theologians espouse is too one-dimensional. In the evangelical view of the Reformation the aim of salvation lies in overcoming the basic contradiction between God and man; we may call this the vertical dimension or the depth dimension, whichever we prefer. In liberation theology the aim of political praxis is to overcome the antithesis between the existing unjust social system and the one to follow; we may call this the horizontal dimension or the breadth dimension. In an eschatological interpretation of history both aims are valorized. Holistic salvation is both other-worldly and this-worldly, present and future, somatic and spiritual, personal and social, religious and secular, historical and eschatological. Persons cannot be saved minus their world. Thus, *liberation* is not a new word *for* salvation; it *is* salvation under the ambiguous conditions of history. The kingdom of God does not limit its arrival to the realm of conscience, as though some totally other rule holds sway in the social sphere. Reinhold Niebuhr's dichotomy of "moral man and immoral society" has tended to split the functions of God's eschatological rule in history into two separate orders of existence, the personal and the social. This dualistic view can be replaced, as did Paul Tillich, by a holistic notion of the multi-dimensional unity of the kingdom of God.

Although salvation includes the social, political, and economic dimensions of life, there still remains the fact that the individual *qua* individual stands as a naked sinner before God. This was the haunting problem for Luther. Even if a person were living in a perfect society, not marked by gross injustice, inequality, poverty, oppression, and disease, there remains the inner space of existential concern as the solitary individual stands alone before God—a lost and condemned sinner. If a person is sorely vexed by problems of anxiety, guilt, sin, death, and meaninglessness, even the rosiest utopia—heaven on earth—would not fill the need of such a wretched soul. There are numerous accounts of a person "gaining the whole world and losing his own soul." Nothing can fill the void in the inner life except the satisfying verdict of God himself, "You are justified!"[13]

Justification may not be the "generative theme" of our epoch, yet despite interesting variations there is a continuing thread of meaning

that links together Paul, Augustine, Luther, Barth, and Tillich.   It
would be arrogant to assert, as some do, that modern man cannot be
reached by the message of justification, because his problem lies elsewhere.   At least in theology the Pauline-Lutheran concept of justification has the merit of highlighting that salvation is by grace alone, that it
presupposes nothing meritorious in the human condition, and that its
validity depends on Christ alone, not on any change for the better in
man.   The very heart of the message of justification *sola fide* is the
flaming truth concerning the priority and paradoxicality of God's grace.
This is scarcely a truth which one outgrows by coming of age.

Reformation theology has centered its attention on the biblical story
of salvation.   God alone is the subject of all saving activity.   Both in its
Lutheran and Calvinist versions the doctrine of salvation has been
monergistic.   Salvation is what God has done; man can relate to it only
in a posture of radical receptivity.   The classic slogans of the Protestant
Reformation—*sola gratia, sola fide, propter Christum*—leave no ambiguity whatsoever on this matter.   They still qualify the one message of
salvation by which the church stands or falls.   For the individual they
spell out the message of forgiveness of sins, that message which alone
can soften the terrors of conscience that attack the core of personal
integrity and wholeness.   The gospel of the forgiveness of sins is addressed to individual persons; it is a matter of existential experience.
To turn it into an ethical imperative, a religious exercise, or any political
praxis is to legalize or moralize the gospel.   Just as Luther protested the
heresy of the late-medieval church which made salvation dependent on
the right kind of religious and moral activity, we have every reason to be
watchful against any reduction of the gospel to the right kind of political
ideology and praxis.   The gospel gets converted into law when reduced
to a set of demands.   The divine indicative then becomes an ethical
imperative subject to human strategies and political tactics.

In liberationist writings the "gospel" represents the ideal state of
affairs, which hopefully will come about some day, and for which we
ought to fight with all our might and mane.   When this happens, the
gospel is no longer a gift but a demand.   We hear loose language about
the demands of the gospel which prescribe for Christians the right kind
of liberating praxis to which they ought to commit themselves.   The

future kingdom comes about through a synergism of divine grace and good works, in this case the right kind of political praxis. The notes of *sola gratia* and *sola fide* are simply not sounded, albeit perhaps for fear they might lead to a salvation by "cheap grace" and thus take the pressure off of Christians to do something concrete to change the social situation.

The gospel gives, the law demands. Unity is one of the gifts of the gospel. Unity, though, is also a demand of the law in order to achieve a just society. But what about the gospel which declares that people are one even though they are seriously divided by race and sex and status? Liberation theologians say that such a gospel is a myth that works to the advantage of the oppressor class. There is no real unity as long as class conflict between rich and poor continues. There is no good news of unity; there is only the law which drives the church to seek unity and to work to overcome the division between rich and poor. What is the gospel, then, prior to the end of the class conflict, or the race conflict, or the sex conflict? Is it only a goad to action? Is it only a goal to be achieved? Or is there already now a real presence of unity in the midst of situations of obvious conflict? Will the gospel become true when we reach the goal of unity, or is it already at work in spite of the distance between the promises of God and the facts of experience? Is there a real presence of the gospel before the arrival of the final kingdom?

According to the message of justification by grace alone, we can already celebrate and practice a unity of brothers and sisters in Christ. We can already declare that in Christ there is no East or West, no rich or poor, no slave or free man, no male or female, no Jew or Greek, no Black or white, no Brahman or pariah, no prince or pauper. None of these distinctions counts as the ultimate mark of human identity. Yet this fact is not a self-evident truth. It is a gift of the gospel already shared as a datum of eschatological salvation even prior to its actualization in history and in spite of the ambiguities of present social reality. Works-righteousness can destroy the gospel, not only in the forms of piety which Luther opposed, but also in modern forms of revolutionary theory. Eschatology is reduced to ethics. The kingdom of God is removed to the future as a goal to be attained by the right kind of ethical action. The gospel is not thought of as a reality in our history, prior to human action, present in the person and ministry of Jesus Christ. Whether we speak of the gospel of justification or the gospel of the kingdom of God, neither the works of personal righteousness nor the works of political liberation avail in building a staircase to heaven.

This paradoxical message of justification declares that it is the sinner who is justified before God, prior to any change for the better in his sinful condition and in spite of the fact that he can point to no inherent quality that puts him in the situation of grace. It is truly liberating for an individual to know, even in a revolutionary struggle, that there is simply nothing inside of him or within his control by which he can be acceptable before God. Yet justification happens, received through faith alone and solely on account of Christ. The message of justification is the answer to the question of what it is which promises grace, what we can really rely on in the ultimate judgment, what will relieve the bitter accusation of conscience, who can make enemies become friends, who can convert a heart of stone, who can offer the assurance of eternal life. Jesus Christ is the flaming center of this message. Justification in his name is valid prior to the works of the regenerate heart or the liberated soul; it is valid in spite of every human failure. Any qualification of this priority and this paradox leads to the synergistic heresy and the legalization of the gospel. This note of unconditional grace has been silenced in the theology of liberation.

The theology of liberation is so afraid of the idea of an "outside deity" that any language of faith or theology which is not plugged into the historical process and the concrete present is dismissed as docetic. The "other side" of God which conceals the mystery of his being tends to be overlooked in the interest of his public manifestations. The motif of the hidden God is collapsed into a doctrine of historical revelation. Yet, the *deus absconditus* is a motif that points to the abysmal aspect of God's life that keeps it shrouded in mystery. It provokes awe; it calls for no particular praxis. There is a transmoral dimension in religious experience not convertible into ethical action or political praxis. God is not always up and doing; he also rests on the Seventh Day in the mystery of his own being. The motifs of mystery and divine transcendence become abbreviated in liberation theology, sometimes being totally obliterated in a radical reduction of God to the dialectics of the historical process.   The phenomena of religious experience which Rudolf Otto, Gerardus van der Leeuw, and Mircea Eliade have illuminated such as the *mysterium tremendum et fascinosum*, are not elements of liberation theology.   A number of explanations for this might be offered, the most obvious being that liberation theology, particularly in its Latin American variant, moves to a great extent within the framework of Marxist categories.   In face of the Marxist critique of religion, Christian apologetics must prove that the Christian faith is equally committed to the historical transformation of reality, not in terms of abstract religious rhetoric but concrete political praxis.   The impact of this alliance is to press religion into the straightjacket of political humanism, the idea of transcendence being consequently flattened out and confined to a "negative dialectic" in the material course of history.

The reduction of theology to the linear horizon of history leads to a selective narrowing of biblical eschatology to its utopian function.   This means that the symbols of hope in biblical eschatology are used to picture a promising future *in* history, but not a fulfilling future *of* history.   Liberation theologians reject every idealistic construct which locates the meaning and goal of history above and beyond the historical process.   For this reason the redefinition of transcendence in an ontology of the future, as proposed by Pannenberg and Moltmann, is looked upon as a relic of idealism.   As Gutierrez says, "One must be extremely careful not to replace a Christianity of the Beyond with a Christianity of the Future."[14]   The priority of the eschatological future kingdom is repudiated by the liberation theologians in the interest of an incarnational presence that creates the future by negating present negativities. Here eschatology becomes so thoroughly immanentized that it fails to express the transcendence of God's sovereign Lordship over history.   It is not seen that eschatology can suggest a new categoreal scheme for conceiving the being of God as the power of the transcendent future, preserving both his involvement in history and his relatedness to it.

The same defect surfaces in the idea of sin. Sin is a religious concept that represents the quality of a person's relationship to God.   Liberation theology is right in broadening the concept of sin to include the social dimension, but its view nevertheless remains rather shallow.   Sin is basically a lack of original righteousness (*carentia iustitiae originalis*), a classical definition that points to a false relationship with God. Sin is concupiscence, the driving tendency of the human heart to curve in on itself manifested as rebellion against God. Some of the richest pictures of sin in the Bible and the classical tradition are blurred in liberation theology. Sin provokes the wrath of God; it is slavery to Satan; it is a state of spiritual death; it is a disease of the whole person—a sickness unto death. It is a state of corruption so profound that the elimination of poverty, oppression, disease, racism, sexism, classism, capitalism, etc., does not alter the human condition of sinfulness in any fundamental way.

Liberation theology is frequently critical of the interpretation of the human condition that runs from Paul, Augustine, and Luther to Barth and Tillich. This interpretation seems to be too subjective, individualistic, and introspective, and at the same time too abstract, ahistorical and other-worldly. However, the Pauline-Lutheran use of absolute categories in depicting our common human sinfulness and alienation from God seems to me more realistic than the relative mediating categories of the liberation thinkers. There is a transcendent dimension of contradiction which dominates all humanity and cuts across every division between classes, sexes, and races. There is no liberation from this universal human condition through social and political praxis of whatever magnitude. In fact, when this fundamental estrangement is cloaked purely in categories of racial or socio-economic analysis, the controlling ideology produces idolatry—man-made gods. Then the real situation of man in the world is covered up. It is the abiding task of Christianity to unmask the illusions that afflict human existence and to expose the pretentions of false offers of salvation.

Sin, death, and the power of the demonic are operative in history to such an extent that nothing less than an apocalyptic revolution of history—not merely a liberation process in history—can bring about such a radical change in man and his society as to eliminate the conditions that give rise to injustice, brutality, and greed. The utopian vision is important and fruitful in society, but it is limited by an infinite distance between what comes about in history through the actions of man and what God does for history through the ministry of Christ. We accept the insight of the liberation theologians that the doctrine of salvation cannot be aimed at man in detachment from his society. That is a truth the missionary implications of which we have only begun to explore. However, the separation of man from God, expressed in the story of the fall, is not going to be overcome once the separation of society into classes is eliminated. Liberation theologians blunt the issue when they too readily accept the definition of the human predicament offered by Marxist ideology. It is true that every person is infected by the sin that separates humanity into classes, but this infection is not the same thing as the universal solidarity of humanity in the structure of sin against God.

Salvation as liberation tends to place the message of eternal life beyond death under a cloud of suspicion. Perhaps it is felt that a moratorium must be placed on this aspect of the church's proclamation, because no way has yet been found to cleanse it of its past ideological function of consoling the poor of this world with promises of riches in the next. Many Christians have come to feel that pious talk about eternal life in a death-dealing system is to make it sound like so much "pie in the sky by and by."

The issue of personal death and hope for eternal life is not, however, a phenomenon of a primitive consciousness, nor is it an opiate created by the ruling class to compensate for hardships in an unjust social order. The problem of death and dying which existentialism has thematized cannot be disposed of by rosy pictures of a future racially harmonious, classless, and nonsexist society. The Marxist philosopher, Milan Machoveč, makes the point: "I do not know, for example, how to deal with death in a Marxist way. I know that . . . on this all too human point the Christian tradition has achieved more than . . . Marxist atheism."[15] The eschatological pictures of the final judgment, the resurrection of the dead, and eternal life should be seen as having power retroactive to these times before the last. They have eschatological relevance for the individual facing the question of the ultimate destiny of life. They also have ethical significance in denouncing those forces that work death and destruction in history, as well as in announcing an ultimate future kingdom which even now quickens the imagination to seek ever greater approximations in this world. Neither the eschatological source of ethics nor the ethical praxis of eschatology should be left marooned without the other.   Otherwise eschatology becomes an escape from history, and ethics is reduced to political humanism.

Liberation theology lays an ambitious program on the church for the construction of society and the promotion of human welfare.   There lies a danger, however, in its conception of the church's relation to the world.   In seeking the disestablishment of Christianity from the old order of Christendom, the question to be asked is whether it seeks a new Constantinianism of the socialist left.   The breakup of one form of culture-Christianity can easily give way to a new in which a hidden triumphalism undergirds assumptions about the church's use of power in the world.   The problem with a new left-wing Constantinianism is that while it appears so attractive today, it may become the source of organized oppression tomorrow.   If the church joins the political praxis of those who seek the overthrow of the existing order, where will it stand in the post-revolutionary situation?   How will it enjoy its success?   Has it dug for itself a political grave for the future?   Has it committed itself to be the priest of a new establishment?   Has it become a prisoner of its own political good luck, so that it makes "peace" and "justice" into an ideology for a world that is still badly split down the middle?

We offer no defense for the crimes against humanity committed in the name of the traditional two-kingdoms doctrine.   The other extreme, however, is a lack of realism about the power of the church effectively to translate its message of salvation into a liberation praxis that transforms the fundamental conditions of human life.   The coming of the new man in a new society, enthusiastically announced by some Maoist Christians, is a prospect which serious believers will take with a grain of salt—all the more so in face of the sobering statistic that sixteen million Chinese are sitting in jail.   How new is a "new world" that cannot tolerate a rich pluralism of expressions which stand both pro and con in respect to the established political system?

A theology of the kingdom of God must coordinate the immanental and transcendental dimensions of God's relation to history.   Whereas the fulfillment of history lies beyond the temporal categories of an existence that ends in death, there is a present reality of that fulfillment which can be enjoyed wherever the miracle of the kingdom is received through faith, hope, and love.   If evangelical theology has been too transcendental, liberation theology tends to be too immanentalist, the one striving for what lies beyond history, the other striving for what lies within it.

THE MISSION OF LIBERATION

1976! That was the year of America's bicentennium. The Post Office issued a special stamp with the slogan: "Proclaim Liberty Throughout the Land." Church conventions were held under the same banner: "Proclaim Liberty!" The theme of liberty rings a bell, not only for the heirs of the American Revolution, but also for the heirs of the Reformation. Liberty was one of Luther's favorite terms, found eloquently in his great classic, *A Treatise on Christian Liberty*. In this writing he stated: "A Christian man is a perfectly free lord of all, subject to no one. A Christian man is a perfectly dutiful servant of all, subject to everyone." Luther was echoing the words of Paul: "Although I am free, I make myself the servant of all."[16]

What does the freedom of the gospel have to do with the *liberté* of the French Revolution and of the Founding Fathers of the American Constitution? What does Martin Luther's liberty of the Christian man have to do with the summer dream of Martin Luther King who shouted, "Free at last! Free at last! Thank God, I'm free at last"? What does the freedom for which Christ sets us free have to do with the "kingdom of freedom" in the vision of Karl Marx? What does Lincoln's "new birth of freedom" have to do with the liberation movements shooting up around the world in the pursuit of justice, equality, freedom, and dignity? The great highway that runs from the airport to downtown Nairobi, Kenya, is called *Uhuru—freedom*, a word that has electrified a continent seeking deliverance from its colonial bondage.

Freedom is indivisible. Christian freedom is not totally different from the liberty and liberation for which in some way all people are longing. Every freedom ultimately has its source in the realm of God's own freedom. The mission of liberation to which Christians are called is not to be confused with counterfeit claims to liberty and the thousand and one pseudo-liberation movements. Every crime in the book has been committed in the name of freedom. For this reason, as Christianity links its mission to liberation as the "generative theme" of our epoch, it must be sure that it does not jump on the bandwagon of every movement in the world that uses the jargon of liberation. We need a theology of the signs of the times, but we are also called to test the spirits. This is mission in the form of critical relevance. If we are serious about the freedom of the gospel, we must boldly spell it out in terms of liberation. We must oppose with prophetic power the social demons of our time. If we love the salvation freedom we have freely received in Christ, we must look for signs of its realization in the liberating work God is doing in history. These signs of liberation are anticipations of the complete salvation summed up in Christ.

The mission of liberation has its source in the gospel of freedom. It is strange that "liberation" has become a word of terror for many modern Christians who see the wolf of revolutionary violence hiding inside the sheep's clothing of liberation movements. When frightened by revolutionary freedom, such Christians are tempted to retrench behind a wall which separates faith and culture. They look for freedom in their faith, in subjective piety or private conscience, retreating from the line where the worldly struggles for freedom and dignity take place. They turn the mission of Christ inward, locking it up in a cult of self-centered piety where the word of God is permitted to vibrate in the souls of religious people. Unable to join a movement for liberation, they reach a mission stalemate, no longer able to tangle with the social demons of our time. The question is whether we can keep the tension between the upward line of faith and the forward line of mission on the model of their intersection in the person of Jesus Christ. To separate these two lines leads to a travesty of mission in which Christian freedom is locked up in the depths of subjective feeling, unrelated to liberation in historical events. Jesus Christ is the ground and the power of both personal freedom and political liberation. If this is not the case, the Christ of faith has been reduced to half a Lord who is no longer the Lord of lords and the exorcist of worldly demons. The liberation movements of our time are not running on a forward line of their own, outside the history of God in the world. Secular history on its own does not exist; all history is the history of God in the fight for human liberation.

There is no mission without a message. Evangelical believers often complain that when churches push the mission of liberation too hard, the message becomes watered down and scarcely Christian anymore. It is well to remind ourselves that the mission of liberation is not the latest invention of liberalism or secularized Christianity. It belongs to the message itself. Getting the message straight is the essence of being orthodox. Similarly, orthopraxis means getting on the right track of mission. The greatest danger is a divorce of praxis from theory, of mission from message, of morality from faith.

Being straight on the message is perhaps the most important first step in rethinking the Christian mission today. The question of strategy and tactics comes second. When the World Council of Churches met in Nairobi, Kenya, in 1975, the section that drew the greatest interest was on "Confessing Christ Today." Although the other sections dealing with human development, the quest for unity, the struggles for justice, education for liberation, interreligious dialogue, and nation-building were of utmost urgency and timeliness, the delegates displayed sound judgment in focusing on Christ, the flaming center of meaning and hope for the world.

The original Ten Commandments were given to Israel as guidelines for life within the framework of its covenant with Yahweh. We need something like the Ten Commandments to guide the Christian community today in seeking a practical expression of its gospel message.

1. The church shall preach no other message of freedom than that which is absolutely essential to the *being* of every person. The gospel of freedom is as ontologically radical as possible, because it liberates a person at the roots of being, at the level of original sin and righteousness, by putting one in touch with the ground and source of all being, the Father Almighty, maker of heaven and earth.

2. The church shall preach the *love* of God as the power of unconditional acceptance, with no strings attached. The message declares the loving will of God to accept people as they are. People are free to love only if they have first been loved; otherwise they are caught in the vicious circle of hate.

3. The church shall not treat its message as something old that needs to be protected, as though it were a museum to house some treasured antiques. Rather, the gospel is always *new* and fresh everyday, like the news in the morning paper, not a bag of old laws and doctrines.

4. The church shall remember that the message is for *all* the people, not the select few who because of ethos or ethnos live inside favored enclaves. The message is universally valid.

5. The church shall remember that its message is not of its own making, a product of its own strength of reason or imagination. It is a gift of divine *revelation*. It is liberating to know that we simply receive the message by faith and that it is hidden from the worldly wise.

6. The church must remember that the message itself is the *power* of God unto salvation. It is *dynamis*—dynamite. It may seem weak by worldly standards, but God's power was revealed in the weakness of Christ on the cross—under a mask of contradiction. This frees the church from the temptation to believe that seeking and grabbing power is the way to the victory of the kingdom of God.

7. The church should celebrate the message to the *glory* of God, even when it seems to be good for nothing. The message makes us free to glorify God with our lives, even when it cannot promise us a better job, peace of mind, inner radiance, positive thoughts, or the like.

8. The church shall make sure the message enfolds the *end* of life. It brings the word of *eternal life*, the last thing of possible human concern. It is an eschatological message of life and death.

9. The church shall deliver the message for the totality of life in all its dimensions. It is a message for the whole person, including what we are *doing* with our minds and bodies. We are to be doers of the word—doing the truth, doing justice, doing peace. The nature of Christian ethics is to explore the doing that is fitting in light of what God has done in Jesus Christ.

10. Finally, the church shall remember that it is compelled to "go and tell" the deeds of God *to all the nations*. Therefore, the message is ecumenical in the broadest sense. We are placed on alert to undertake the impossible mission of reaching the world with the good news of its own fulfilling meaning and goal in Jesus Christ.

If these ten imperatives frame our understanding of the gospel message, the wall of separation that hampers the church from linking its gospel of freedom to the liberation process in history can no longer stand. There is nothing to the right and nothing to the left, nothing in politics, nothing in the church, that can either claim to merit the grace of

God or exempt itself from his judgment. No separation! Our mission is to make a mess of the line that runs between the church and the world, by mixing the gospel into every sector of life. The kingdom game is not played by the rules of the church, on its field and inside church limits. There is no "out of bounds" for the ministry of the church.

We have underscored the essential attributes of the gospel message in order to make sure that everything we do on the circumference of mission emanates from the flaming center of faith in Christ. If we are going to broaden the mission to include human development, education for liberation, ideological criticism, and nation-building, then these gospel attributes will equip the church to be faithful to her own Lord. It is almost too good to be true that we have received a message with these marks: radical freedom, unconditional love, good news, universal validity, divine revelation, power for salvation, the glory of God, the end of life, the norming of human action, meaning, and direction to world history. Only this message can liberate mission to a new era of global dimensions.

Because we have this message this is no time for ecclesiastical retrenchment or retirement from mission. There is only one way to go and that is forward. We are not helpless. Alongside this message we have multitudes of men and women willing to serve, we have money and material, we have theology and technology. We are without excuse if we do not quicken the pace and enlarge the scope of mission in our time.

BROADENING THE HORIZON OF MISSION

The mission of the church is to liberate groups and nations from their ethnocentric spirit of divisiveness and from the idolatrous elevation of their own particularity to the level of ultimate significance. The unity of mankind is divided by wars between nations, races, and religions. Every day brings new accounts of horrors between Catholics and Protestants in Ireland, Palestinians and Christians in Lebanon, whites and Blacks in South Africa, Greeks and Turks in Cyprus. The church carries a message of unity to all the nations. This places a high premium on the ecumenical search for unity among the churches themselves, if the churches are to be a more expressive symbol of the coming unity of all mankind. The mission of the church is to pursue ways and means of incorporating the eschatological unity of humankind in the kingdom of God into concrete situations of conflict, misunderstanding, and mutual hostility. How can a divided Christianity do this in a credible way, each party busy with its own tedious agenda?

There is a sinful tendency in human nature which drives to narrow parochialism, seeking security in closed systems that mirror the image of one's own ego. The proclamation of the gospel liberates people from the demonic powers of nature and history that enthrall, mystify, dominate, and suppress. The church should seize the kairotic moment to link the secular quest for interdependence among the nations to the ecumenical unity growing in the churches. A particular church body has to decide whether its own denominational identity has to die in order to be raised up as an ecclesial sign of the unity which God is forging in society at large. If a Lutheran mission is at work in a so-called Catholic country, it has to decide whether to build a parallel church structure, thus extending and perpetuating Lutheranism as a denomination, or to die to itself in order to be resurrected as an auxiliary of the existing church's mission, thus preserving and nourishing the image of unity in the body of Christ.

The gospel of Jesus Christ is the announcement of the unity which God has in store for all mankind. The mission of the church is to take this promise of unity and use it to build community in the midst of people of various religious and cultural persuasions. Christians must coexist with neighbors who reserve their loyalties for other divinities and ideologies. They have a mission to these neighbors quite apart from making them Christians, and that is to build up the highest quality of life in common human community. Without relinquishing one iota of their own commitment, Christians will broaden common understanding, cooperating and sharing with all their neighbors of whatever religious or ideological loyalty. Jesus Christ liberates Christians to explore the resources of every tradition which can contribute to the common good. Christians in India and Japan tell of the personal and communal values which their own societies have received through Hinduism and Buddhism. A Christian does not strengthen his own identity by negating these values; he only succeeds in weakening the quality of the common life.   Christians in Africa tell us that the first missionaries were too hasty in rejecting everything connected with the traditional religions, including not only idols and witchcraft, but also drums and dancing.   More importantly, missionaries could have found among Africans a sense of community more suitable to the biblical concept of the church than the Western spirit of individualism they brought with them.   The mission now has to go back and retrieve what is essential to African identity, in order to advance the gospel in concrete forms of thought and communal life true to African experience.   Christians in Eastern Europe also testify that socialism has discovered ways of implementing justice and equality that deserve their support, in spite of the fact that too often individual freedom is sacrificed to bureaucratic conformity.   All of these examples show that Christians can learn from their neighbors and join the common quest for wider and deeper forms of human community.

The church's mission must also take up the challenge of educators like Paulo Freire and Ivan Illich who make a sharp distinction between education for liberation and education for domestication.[17]   Those familiar with Lutheran categories might be helped to understand this distinction if they remember the difference between law and gospel.   Education under the law would be legalistic and therefore domesticating; education under the gospel would be evangelical and therefore liberating.   Freire, to be sure, writes like an antinomian, as though it would be possible to have an education for liberation without domesticating elements.   The antinomian believes he can live his life solely by the gospel without the guidelines of the law.   Nevertheless, as the distinction between law and gospel can be useful if their functions in real experience are not separated, so also the distinction between liberation and domestication can be helpful if we bear in mind that only in utopia will there be pure and undomesticated freedom.

The Portuguese word *conscientizacao* is Freire's chosen term to denote a truly liberating style of education.   In English its closest equivalent is "consciousness-raising," with the difference that the Portuguese word more clearly conveys the connotation of "critical" awareness.   The chief purpose of this process is to make human beings into personal subjects critically aware and actively engaged in the making of history. This is particularly urgent for poor and oppressed people who are usually cast in the role of passive objects pushed around in the interest of their oppressors.

Oppressed people will not be set free by their oppressors; they must liberate themselves through transforming action and thus create a new situation in which the oppressor-oppressed contradiction is overcome. The goal of liberating education is the humanization of all people and the appearance of a "new man in a new society."

Education for domestication treats people like animals. Domesticating education treats persons like objects to be possessed or manipulated. Freire calls it the "banking" concept of education. In this approach people are taught to enter the existing system and move up the ladder, not to question or imagine ways fundamentally to change the system. Liberating education makes people into free subjects; it is fulfilling, humanizing, and transforming. Domesticating education is alienating, dominating, repressive, and depersonalizing; it makes people apathetic, subservient slaves of the ready-made world.

The church has always been involved in education as a form of its mission. In many lands it has been ahead of the state in teaching people how to read and write, the skills of a trade, the arts of a more civilized way of life. In light of Freire's pedagogical theory, however, the church has too often followed the easier model of domesticating education. This has placed the church on the side of indoctrination, imposing external authorities and paternalistic screening of information deemed useful to the less fortunate. This approach makes people automatons, parrots, or duplicates of approved models often imported from a more "advanced" culture. The church too has been somewhat afraid of the freedom that people might gain in the liberating approach. It is more safe to treat people like children or animals, lest in thinking for themselves they make mistakes and get hurt. Education as the practice of freedom is risky. The future is open and there is no telling what the people will decide is good for them. Freire calls this approach "problem-posing." In a new situation the teacher can ask questions and pose problems, or he can bring answers and solutions that have worked in other times and places. But if the future is open, if society is incomplete and man is unfinished, education must help people to look forward and move ahead into *terra incognita.*

Freire paints a totally negative picture of domesticating education. It can spell repression and bondage. But there is a positive aspect that the church dare not overlook in its own educational approach. While Freire's model points people to revolutionary futurity, it does little to water the roots of identity that lie in the past. It is suicide for Christianity to neglect its past, for the past bears the words of promise and the voice of prophecy. Freire operates with a humanistic model in which the truth lies within each person, only to be released through the midwifery of a Socratic teacher; he does not employ the biblical model in which the truth has appeared in history as a subject of remembered events, historical reports, and proven traditions that must be handed on to the next generation. Nevertheless, Freire's pedagogy of the oppressed brings out a liberating, critical, political, revolutionary, and future-oriented aspect of education on which the church has been lax. Freire's onesideness can serve to challenge the church to reevaluate its role in education around the world, lest by default it covertly work in cahoots with the dominant elites.

The church in mission can no longer afford to becloud its vision with evangelistic rhetoric and ignore what the Bible calls "the powers and the principalities" or what the modern idiom refers to as "the structures of injustice." This is the most difficult area in which to spell out the implications for mission, because it is always a high-risk venture for the church to contend with powers that are ruled by "the god of this world." Nonetheless, it is even more dangerous for the church to seek an asylum for its evangelistic mission in exchange for silence concerning the structures that determine the political and economic conditions of ordinary citizens. If the church takes a conservative hands-off attitude, it actually reinforces the structures of violence and exploitation. The sectarian option of radical withdrawal from the emerging universal culture of technology and bureaucracy leads to the same neutralizing of the Christian contribution to modern life. The church is left with either of several options, which liberation theologians refer to as reformist as over against revolutionary. The reformist model calls for Christians to be involved in society at all levels, improving it a step at a time, educating public opinion, working to make the political and legal systems more responsive to the needs of the people, and being watchdogs in the interest of civil and religious liberties. The assumption is that society can be modified in important ways so as not merely to rearrange things to the advantage of the existing power structures.

The revolutionary model looks upon the reformist Christian as a kind of Quisling. The reformist ideal is one of peaceful cooperation with the existing order, making a positive contribution to society while advancing private interests, and always collaborating with those who make the rules of the game. Furthermore, the reformist approach never really changes things, in spite of all the talk about change. The revolutionary works and prays for the collapse of the established system and for the emergence of a new one in which qualitative changes will be reflected at the grassroots level, especially for the oppressed and exploited.

Many Christians seriously believe that they must identify with the revolutionary vanguard who openly challenge the structures of injustice. The problem with this posture is that when revolutionary praxis threatens the power elites, the movement is squashed by imprisonment or exile, as in the case of Paulo Freire's own experience in Brazil. It would seem, therefore, that whereas the revolutionary approach may be chosen by individual Christians, the church's own strategy for confronting structures of injustice will more modestly advance on the reformist model. When both approaches are simultaneously pursued in the same country, enormous tensions are bound to arise within the church, even leading to schism, as recently occurred among Lutherans in Chile.

In any case, it seems clear today that the church's mission must include more conscious participation in struggles for liberation, in critique of society, and in effective action to change the structures of injustice. It is also clear that the churches have a long way to go to overcome the widespread image of Christianity as a massive reactionary force more or less in league with the powers that be. It is even doubtful that the church has at the present time the resources in its own structures and theological curricula to move its mission to the frontlines of struggle for justice and freedom.

On another front the church in mission will give expression to its appointment as stewards of the whole creation. The meaning of Christian stewardship has been expanded by the new ecological awareness. The traditional concept of stewardship has been church-centered, a challenge to the laity to give their time, talents, and treasures *to the church*. Stewardship has meant church finance and fund raising; it has meant tithing and charity. The appeal has been too subjectivistic, individualistic, and moralistic, and as a consequence irrelevant to the conditions of modern life. The ecological crisis has prompted the church to recover a holistic concept of stewardship from the biblical theology of covenant and creation.

From the Old Testament we learn that stewardship is not based on an individualistic ethic of rightly motivated individuals, but is built into the law of the whole covenant community. Stewardship stems from the election of a whole people and from their responsibility for the whole of life. Christianity has tended to place stewardship under the category of charity; it belongs rather under justice. Giving to a neighbor in need is to share with him what really belongs to God. We all have an equal share in God's patrimony. We are all his stewards. "The earth is the Lord's and the fulness thereof."[18] It is sub-biblical to think that our stewardship is a matter of mercy to the less fortunate, rather than a simple matter of dealing justly with our fellow human beings.

As we broaden this concept of stewardship it takes on public and political dimensions.[19] Thus, when our generation faces a staggering gap between wealthy and poor people, between rich and poor nations, that becomes a problem of stewardship. Closing this gap is perhaps the most important item on the new agenda of church stewardship. "Bread for the World" is a movement that recognizes the urgency of healing this great wound in the body of mankind.

In addition to being a redemptive use of wealth, stewardship is the right use of the power of science and technology for human good. The survival of humanity at a qualitatively high level of life depends on the care of the earth. As offspring of the new Adam we should care for the earth, God's gift of a garden to all the descendants of the first Adam. Mission as stewardship deals with such seemingly secular issues as the evils of waste, conspicuous consumption, economic growth as an end in itself without regard to its effects on the environment, water, air, food, and soil pollution. Christian stewardship places us on the side of all people who fight against the forces that lead to decay and destruction. Christianity carries a vision of a new heaven and a new earth, and its mission is to make that dream come true as far as possible under the conditions of our earthly existence.

As stewards of the whole creation, we are also to care for our bodies as temples of the Holy Spirit. We cannot leave that out of our gospel proclamation. A Western scholar once asked an old Caledonian whether it was not the idea of the soul that Christianity had brought to the island. "No," came the reply, "we already knew about that; what you have given to us is the notion of the body."[20] What happens in our bodies has profound repercussions on the spiritual and mental dimensions of life and health. Stewardship of the body means that churches should become institutes of life and health, liberating the whole person for joy in Christ and love for the neighbor.

NOTES

1. Enrique Dussel, *History and the Theology of Liberation* (MaryKnoll: Orbis Books, 1976).

2. José Míguez-Bonino, *Doing Theology in a Revolutionary Situation* (Philadelphia: Fortress, 1975).

3. Liberation theology makes its connection with Marxism not only by way of sociological analysis but also by way of the Bible. See for example, Carlos Mesters, *Eden: Golden Age or Goad to Action* (MaryKnoll: Orbis, 1974) and José Miranda, *Marx and the Bible* (MaryKnoll: Orbis, 1974). It bears repeating that Marxism is a Christian heresy rooted in the Old Testament and born in the heartland of the Reformation.

4. Gustavo Gutierrez, *A Theology of Liberation* (MaryKnoll: Orbis, 1973), p. 15.

5. Wolfhart Pannenberg, "Redemptive Event and History," *Basic Questions in Theology*, Vol. I, (Philadelphia: Fortress, 1970), p. 15.

6. The doctrine of God remains perhaps the most underdeveloped aspect of the theology of liberation, but see Juan Luís Segundo's attempt, *Our Idea of God*, Volume III of *A Theology for Artisans of a New Humanity* (MaryKnoll: Orbis, 1974).

7. Paulo Freire, *Pedagogy of the Oppressed* (New York: Herder and Herder, 1970), p. 93.

8. Hugo Assmann, *Theology for a Nomad Church* (MaryKnoll: Orbis, 1975), p. 67.

9. Gustavo Gutierrez, *A Theology of Liberation*, p. 175.

10. *Ibid.*

11. Peter Beyerhaus, *Allen Völkern zum Zeugnis* (Wuppertal: Brockhaus, 1972).

12. See our book on the theology of the body: Carl and LaVonne Braaten, *The Living Temple* (New York: Harper & Row, 1976).

13. See my article, "The Gospel of Justification Sola Fide," *dialog* (Summer, 1976), Vol. 15.

14. Gustavo Gutierrez, *A Theology of Liberation*, p. 218.

15. In Paul Oestreicher, ed., *The Christian Marxist Dialogue* (New York: 1969), p. 127. See also Machoveč, *A Marxist Looks At Jesus* (Philadelphia: Fortress, 1976).

16. 1 Corinthians 9:19.

17. This need has been recognized by the Lutheran World Federation in its sponsorship of a series of consultations on "Theological Presuppositions Implicit in the Current Theories of Education for Domestication or Liberation." At this consultation I delivered a lecture entitled, "The Challenge of Liberation Theology—A Lutheran Perspective," parts of which have been reworked in this chapter.

18. Psalm 24:1.

19. Around 1960 the National Council of Churches sponsored a theological study conference on stewardship. Stewardship was looked at from every conceivable angle. An interesting theological problem became evident in the contrast between contributions offered by two Lutheran theologians. The two theologians were T. A. Kantonen of the former United Lutheran Church and Edgar Carlson of the former Augustana Lutheran Church. Using the Lutheran distinction between law and gospel, Kantonen argued that stewardship belongs not under law but under the gospel. His reasoning was simple and familiar. God has given us the gospel. This grants forgiveness of sins and a new relationship to God. Our response of gratitude follows. This generates stewardship. We give because God has given first. Gratitude is the basic motivation for stewardship. In this concept of stewardship the emphasis is on "right motives." It seems difficult to take objection to this gospel-oriented concept of stewardship.

Edgar Carlson, approaching the issue from another angle, dealt with Gustav Wingren's criticism of Einar Billing's theology. Wingren challenged the idea of placing stewardship within the circle of the gospel, while treating law in a purely negative fashion. Wingren argued that a true interpretation of Luther's theology would place stewardship under the First Article of the Creed, the "law of creation," rather than deriving it solely from the Second Article of the Creed and the "means of grace." Stewardship takes place within the structure of existence. All people, furthermore, and not only grateful believers, are held accountable for their stewardship of life, its duties and responsibilities. Everyone is a steward of God under the law of creation, whether he likes it or not. One is unavoidably a steward—good or bad—of God's creation in one's secular vocation, and not solely on account of one's Christian calling. Thus, not only the motive of giving is important, but the gift itself is important. Even a gift given with great reluctance may have great significance.

The effect of Wingren's proposal is to broaden the meaning of stewardship in line with the biblical concept and with the conditions of modern life. The need is to liberate stewardship from a narcissistic preoccupation with subjective intentions and individualistic feelings, however much they may be clothed in gospel–oriented language. Stewardship for today must be placed within the larger orbit of life in all its dimensions. Our suggestions aim to free the concept of stewardship from its captivity to person–centered and church–centered thinking, and locate it rather in a theology of the world. Cf., *Stewardship in Contemporary Theology*, T. K. Thompson ed., (New York: Association, 1960).

20. The anecdote is recounted by C. A. van Peursen, *Body, Soul, Spirit: A Survey of the Body-Mind Problem* (Oxford: Oxford University Press, 1966), p. 85.